Dedicated to Fellow and Future Earth Riders

Forth to Basics: A Guide to Goin' Off-Grid
(and living more with less)

For information, contact:

David R. Welder
PO Box 414
Osseo, WI 54758

www.forthtobasics.com

Book and cover design by Anniken Fuller (annikencreative.com)
Photography by Dave & Veronica Welder (and others as footnoted)
ISBN 978-1-961026-02-5
Second Edition: January 2024

Published by Pine Run Press
pinerunpress.com

PINE
RUN
PRESS

# FORTH TO BASICS

## A GUIDE TO GOIN' OFF-GRID
### (and living more with less)

### by David R. Welder

# TABLE OF CONTENTS

# INTRODUCTION

If you love to camp, hike, explore and do-it-yourself (DIY), then you're a fellow *"Outsider."* A simpler, off-grid lifestyle could be just the thing you're dreaming of. The lower cost of living and added health benefits far outweigh the occasional discomfort and inconvenience of living off-grid. Well, at least some of us think so!

I first got the off-grid bug while watching Dick Proenneke build his small cabin in remote Alaska. I'm referring to the documentary TV program *Alone in The Wilderness* which has been aired on PBS television for years. Dick single-handedly built his cabin in the late 1960s and filmed the whole process with a hand-held movie camera. As a young fort-builder living in the rural Midwest, I thought to myself *"Whoah, Coool… I wonder if I could do that?"* I wonder no more. *"Thanks Dick!"*

I admit, at the outset, not everyone can seamlessly transition to off-grid living without some loss of comfort and convenience. After all, many of us grew up in climatically-controlled environments with only brief excursions outside of our homes, cars, workplaces, etc. Modern heating and cooling systems have made life much more comfortable, but at what cost? More about that later.

Of course, if everyone left the cities and moved to nature, there would be consequences. If you prefer city life, there are other ways to reduce your individual environmental footprint and cost of living. At the same time, if a few more people could live within nature as stewards of the natural world, then we'd all be better off.

Despite significant reductions in air and water pollution over 50 years and the return of many wild species, it still feels like we're more of an invasive species than stewards of nature. Reduced biodiversity and fossil fuel use are major contributors to our global strife. Whether we like it or not, these problems are not going away anytime soon. My goal is to show others how to reduce their impacts on nature by thinking globally and acting locally.

Let me briefly mention the term *"off-grid,"* which has caught on in recent years. Technically, it means disconnecting from the North American electrical supply grid. For us, it also involves disconnecting from most paid services provided by others. This means:

- No natural gas lines
- No indoor plumbing
- No public water supply system
- No public sewage disposal system
- No waste collection service

Yes this lifestyle involves a bit more daily labor but with a little modern technology, you don't have to sacrifice much of your comfort, convenience and income earning potential. This ain't your *Little House on the Prairie* lifestyle.

You may also need or want to keep connected with others and access useful information on the internet. Therefore, cell phones, a computer and satellite internet connection may be necessary, even key to your success. You can certainly transition all the way back to a 19th-century lifestyle and skip the phone and internet altogether (our Amish neighbors do), but these tools make it easier to maintain an income, pay bills and stay connected.

In the following pages, I will demonstrate how going off-grid can reduce your overall cost of living in monetary terms. The electric grid and its many conveniences have been around for less than a hundred years. Yeah, it's been nice but it ain't been free. Some of us find that the *"old ways"* offer practical and inexpensive options.

The off-grid concept might seem daunting at first, but realize that the vast majority of all humans who have ever lived, did so without instantly-accessible electric power. You too, can rough it in style with this tried-n-true way of life.

By showing how we did it (HWDI), my goal is to provide you with some basics concepts and important details so you can do it yourself (DIY).

By combining old-school knowledge with modern technology, I hope to demonstrate that you can live and work in relative comfort while using (and wasting) less of the planet's finite natural resources, including fossil fuels. My hope is to inspire others to go forth and live simply, sustainably and peacefully… living OF the land rather than OFF the land. 🪙

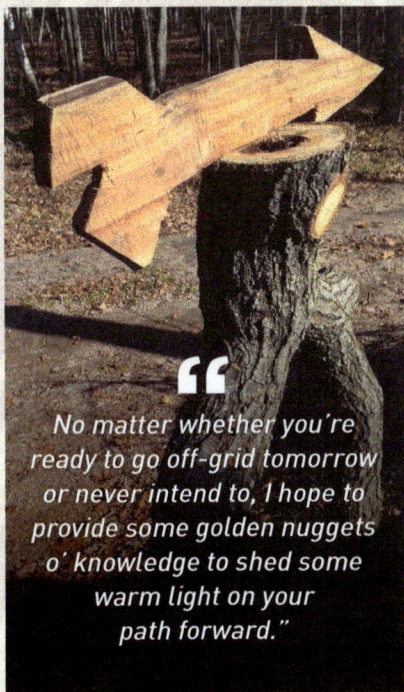

> **"** *No matter whether you're ready to go off-grid tomorrow or never intend to, I hope to provide some golden nuggets o' knowledge to shed some warm light on your path forward."*

# CHAPTER 1

# ARE YOU READY?

*Do we continue with our current paycheck to paycheck situation?*
*— or —*
*Do we pull up roots and make a big change to a simpler existence?*

This is the quandary Veronica and I faced a few years ago. We persevered a long time with the first option but never seemed to save much for retirement. Bills, fees, cons and emergency expenditures ate it all up. Sound familiar? Well, we made the jump, built a new life together and never looked back. Wasn't easy but ahh the rewards!

The following are some things to consider before making that big decision.

Photo: Bruce Christianson

# TAKE STOCK

### First, we took stock of our resources.

Resources include money, land, materials, etc. Whether you have plentiful resources or next to none, just make a list of everything you have. Good credit is also a resource but only if used wisely and sparingly. Debt is not a resource.

### Second, we took stock of our skills.

Red Green said *'If you can't be handsome, at least you can be handy.'* The bottom line is, if you're handy, you can live off-grid. If you cannot wield a hammer without injuring yourself, then this will be a more difficult endeavor (but not an impossible one).

You can learn the basics from books or online tutorials but the best way to learn is to: Just Do. You may fail at times, but will develop skills through practice. And the end result doesn't have to be perfect, just functional. Those who are physically impaired or un-handy can still hire friends, family or a professional contractor.

One big mistake is to expect friends and family to do the work just for beer and cookies! That can work, but only for one day. Whether hiring an extra Hand or simply asking for help...**Before you begin, agree on a Win-Win** (preferably in writing).

# PULL TOGETHER

The saying goes, "Opposites attract." Another saying goes: "Opposites attract divorce lawyers."

The truth, as usual, is somewhere in the middle. Your partner (or partners) can have different hobbies and tastes, but when it comes to living more primitively, you both (or all) gotta be on the same page…or at least on the same chapter. If you both/all love the outdoors and don't mind occasional hardships, then anything's possible.

The stressors of life are bad enough, but the stress of moving and building a new life can shake even strong bonds. You simply can't place too much mental or physical burden on your bunkmate. That burden can result in resentment and conflict which is counterproductive (and a real downer).

Sometimes it's good to spend time apart and do your own thing. It all needs to get done, so just do your part. **When it comes to cooperation, one-plus-one can equal three but one-minus-one still equals zero.**

Below is one of the best pieces of advice I've ever read. Thanks Steve.

*"Don't let something that doesn't matter cause you to lose something that does."*

–Steve Jobs

This is a universal truth that especially applies to interpersonal relations. You can and should debate issues of common interest and concern, but bicker and argue over stupid inconsequential stuff? That's a huge waste of time and no path to contentment. The only thing that an argument ever proved is that there are two or more people in disagreement. Each one of us has the ability to stop it, drop it, and roll.

Also, don't be too proud or stubborn to say, *"Thank You"* and *"I Apologize"* or *"I Was Wrong"*. These are NOT signs of weakness but rather signs of a good person. These simple statements will go a long way toward interpersonal harmony and contentment, no matter where or how you live or love.

*"It is only possible to live happily ever after on a day to day basis."*

– Margaret Bonnano

# PLAN LIKE BEN

Ben Franklin was one of our country's most creative and productive citizens. Without his incredible contributions to the greater good, history would have been written much differently. His lifelong method of planning and prioritization allowed him to direct his efforts towards the most important goals.

Planning is a key practice that will save loads of time and may even help calm your mind. For years I've been following the example of Ben Franklin who set aside time for planning and prioritizing. He did this at the beginning of each day, each week, each month and each year.

Ben accomplished many things in his life and his organizational skills are one of the big reasons. His plan-first philosophy is the basis for the popular Franklin-Covey Books and Daily Planners. In a nutshell, is as follows:

1. Figure out what's most important to you
2. Make goals based on what's most important
3. Routinely schedule your time to work toward those goals

*"By failing to prepare, you are preparing to fail."*
— Benjamin Franklin

I'm not sure about many things, but I am sure that time spent planning is time well spent. Planning saves way more time than it takes to do. How much time does planning take? Not much! My planning schedule when faced with multiple tasks and deadlines: 15 minutes per day, either with coffee in the morning (to prioritize my day) or before bed (to calm my monkey-mind). Additionally, I often spend 15-30 minutes on Sunday night or Monday morning planning the upcoming week. Same thing with the month and year, but I spend more time on those planning sessions.

A powerful (almost magical) thing happens when you write down your goals and plans…your subconscious mind will continue to work out the details even when you're not actively thinking about it. I call this method of planning *"Seeding Your Subconscious."* Sometimes the perfect solution to a complex problem just pops in your head. "Wha?…Yes!" It worked for Ben and definitely works for me!

When things are running smoothly and I only have a few tasks (chop firewood and clean outhouse), I often skip the planning sessions. Then I just pick up the planning habit again when things get more complicated. Even during calmer times, I still ask myself, *"What's the most important thing I can accomplish today?"* Sometimes, the answer is *"chop a face-cord of firewood"* Sometimes, the answer is *"rest,"* or *"explore."*

If you need a jumpstart to your plan, **Appendix A** contains a basic planning checklist for building an off-grid life.

# DO THE MATH

Don't like basic math? That's ok, but I can tell you there's nothing like a recession or financial crisis to motivate you to put pencil to paper!

After 20 years of self-employment, and often just getting by, my work hours suddenly declined and soon living expenses far exceeded income. The first step (after panicking) was to trim any unnecessary expenses. The only *"pork fat"* to trim at this point was the land-line phone service, restaurant dining and cable TV. With no fat left, we continued to feel the financial pressure, so we put pencil to paper, tallied all of our expenses and realized that going off-grid could drastically reduce expenses. Below is a table of our city living expenses (2017)

compared to our current (2022) off-grid living expenses. It shows that our cost of living was cut roughly in half. Granted, much of this was because we no longer had a mortgage or rent payment. Significant reductions in property taxes and electric costs have also helped to keep more money in our pockets.

Now, before I get carried away discussing money, in the next chapter I'll explore our human survival needs and recommend a frugal balance between wants and needs.

| Our Expenses<br>Values are approximate and do not consider inflation. | Before<br>(2017) | After<br>(2022) |
|---|---|---|
| Mortgage Payment | $1050 | $ 0 |
| Property Taxes/Ins. | $ 250 | $ 80 |
| Food | $ 600 | $ 500 |
| Fuel – Autos (2) | $ 200 | $ 80 |
| Fuel – Heating, Cooking, Misc. | $ 60<br>(natural gas) | $ 75<br>(wood, propane, gasoline) |
| Electric/Batteries | $ 150 | $ 10 |
| Wifi | $ 100 | $ 108 |
| Cell Phones (2) | $ 220 | $ 80 |
| Auto Insurance | $ 93 | $ 60 |
| Water and Ice | $ 25 | $ 60 |
| Laundry | $ 10 | $ 20 |
| Trash Disposal | $ 15 | $ 10 |
| Misc Personal* | $ 200 | $ 200 |
| **Total** | **$2973** | **$1283** |

\* *Miscellaneous personal expenses include: clothes, prescriptions, paper products, entertainment, and refreshments. Additional medical, dental, or unforeseen repair work has been omitted.*

# CHAPTER 2

# WHAT DO YOU REALLY NEED?

We've been programmed to believe that we cannot live without certain items and services. Before I detail what you'll need to live off-grid, let's go big-picture and review those things that we all need to survive.

**Rule of 3's for Human Survival:**
An average human can survive without air, water, or food for only a limited time. How long?

    **Air**: 3 minutes
    **Water**: 3 days
    **Food**: 3 weeks

1. Air
2. Water
3. Food
4. Clothing
5. Shelter
6. Fuel
7. Sanitation
8. Rest

Shelter and clothing (portable shelter) are also necessary to maintain proper body temperature. Without adequate clothing and shelter in winter, you'd be lucky to last 3 hours! In addition, you can go without fuel, rest or proper sanitation for days… but what a drag! These are what I consider to be the 8 essentials for human survival:

In our modern world, especially in northern climates, we may need somewhat more than just basic survival essentials. Other needs may include:

9. Tools
10. Electric Power
11. Transportation
12. Communications
13. Income

We'll cover 9 through 13 later, but let's first look at each of the 8 essential human needs and explore how to maintain a sustainable supply of each.

# AIR

The need that we need the most is air, but we often take it for granted. Outdoor air quality in our area is excellent but there's still pollen, mold, dust and fumes to deal with. Folks who struggle with allergies and respiratory problems (like me) pay more attention to pollen counts and air quality warnings.

Even if the outdoor air is good, the air quality inside of your shelter can become tainted if you're careless. The USEPA has long reported that indoor air is typically 3 to 5 times more polluted than outside air. Two causes of poor indoor air quality include toxic mold and VOCs (volatile organic compounds) from building materials (carpets, glues, paints).

Other causes of bad indoor air involve the use of bleach and certain household chemicals. Bleach combined with ammonia or any acidic liquid will kill mold but it produces chlorine gas, chloroform and a lot of other toxic stuff I can't even pronounce. People continue to wind up in the emergency room after cleaning (over-cleaning) with bleach and ammonia... Uff da!

Another common way to taint your air supply is through improper fuel combustion and exhaust ventilation. Scores of people around the world routinely cook over indoor wood, coal or dung fires with little-to-no ventilation. This practice might ensure short-term survival but it's not great for long-term health. So, it's important to have a good chimney and proper ventilation when it comes to any fuel-burning system. Also important are Carbon Monoxide/Fire alarms. They provide a lot of safety and peace of mind for a small cost.

*Don't take air for granted. It's your primary life-line.*

*"I arise in the morning torn between a desire to improve (or save) the world, and a desire to enjoy (or savor) the world. This makes it hard to plan the day."*
– E. B. White

# WATER

Our second most important and immediate need is water – cool, clear water. We all need it every single day for drinking and cooking. Water is also needed for weekly washing of dishes, clothes... and yourself! A good water source is extremely important and will directly impact your lifestyle.

One of the greatest achievements of modern society is the widespread availability of clean water for city and town-dwellers through municipal public water systems. Families who live in rural areas must rely on other sources. We are fortunate to have excellent groundwater but we also utilize bottled water (for drinking) and rainwater (for washing and watering).

### Bottled Water

It sometimes feels like cheating, but we do occasionally purchase bottled water for drinking, cooking and light rinsing. We prefer 1-gallon or 4-gallon containers of spring water. The cost of bottled water currently (2022) starts at around $1.50 per gallon but increases to over $10 per gallon, if you buy individual "teenie-weenie" water bottles.

If you need to purchase a gallon or more per day per person, that can add up fast. The benefit is that we're pretty sure it's safe to drink. No matter how much you have to pay for water, it's still better than sickness or dehydration. For many with tainted water supplies, bottled water is the only viable option for drinking. So, for better or worse, bottled water will continue to be a necessity for some.

### Rainwater and Snow

For washing, our favorite sources are rainwater and melted snow. It takes less than 5 gallons to wash the dishes and the price is right! This water doesn't need to be 100% clean but not green or brown. Just add a few drops of dish soap and let the dishes soak. Later, scrub and rinse with clean, hot water. After a quick wipe-dry or slow air-dry, dishes are "Campsite Clean!"

We use simple eco-friendly dish soap, so watering plants with dirty wash water doesn't hurt 'em. A wee bit of dish soap in the water can even dissuade aphids and other insects from nibbling your veggies.

275-gallon Caged Tote for rainwater collection

Oak rain barrel (previously used for booze)

## How much rainwater can your house's roof provide?

You can estimate how much rainwater can be collected during a 1-inch rainfall if you know the approximate square footage (sf) of your roof.

**Area of roof** (sq ft) x 1.0 inch of rain x 0.62 = gallons of rainwater

### Example of 1.0-inch rain on our small cabin roof:

500 sq ft  x 1.0 x 0.62  = 310 gallons

That's plenty of water to fill 5 drums or 1 tote!

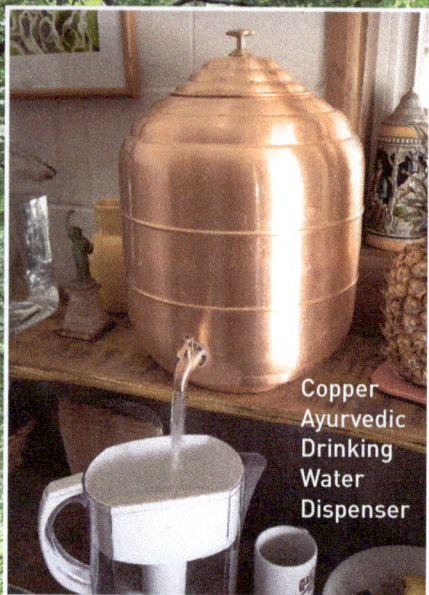

Copper
Ayurvedic
Drinking
Water
Dispenser

## Well Water

We are fortunate to have easily-accessible groundwater 8 feet down, so we were able to reduce our purchased water by installing a simple **sand-point well** with hand powered pitcher pump. No farm fields or industrial activities are located nearby, so the risk of man-made contamination is low. Nevertheless, we test the well water periodically for bacteria and other contaminants. So far, so good!

If you can access good clean well water, then you are lucky-ducks indeed! Depending on where you live in the country, there may be restrictions on installing your own well. Check with state and local regulations. In some cases, you can manually install your own sand-point well. In other areas, you first need a permit. If you are planning to DIY, there are tons of online tips and tutorials.

You might find the perfect location to live, but the groundwater below could be tainted, smelly, rusty, inaccessible or even nonexistent. Darn! There are always options but few are cheap.

If you hire a well-drilling company to install a well, the cost starts at roughly $500 and can rise to $5,000 for deeper or more difficult drilling. I've been inspired by "Earthship" dwellers in bone-dry parts of New Mexico who have found novel and sustainable ways to collect, store, and recycle

enough water to meet their daily needs. If you build your shelter on top of a hill, you're gonna need a deeper well. If you build at the valley bottom you could get flooded out, or away. Best to locate your shelter (and water well) somewhere in between. Whatever you do, never install a well downhill from an outhouse or septic system. While it's true that astronauts recycle their pee, this should be avoided!

Installing sand-point well

Hand Pump

# FOOD

We live near farm country, so when it comes to readily available and inexpensive food, we are better off than most. Locally-sourced veggies, meats and dairy are available from the grocery store or directly from farmers. In addition, we plant an annual garden which provides many pounds of fresh produce. We tend to purchase less expensive vegetables at the store (onions, potatoes, carrots) and grow more expensive, perishable vegetables in our garden, especially leafy greens and herbs.

If you track or estimate your current yearly food costs, you might be surprised by what you find. According to the Bureau of Labor Statistics (2020), the average American spent $200-500 on food per month. It's still possible to survive on $200 worth of food per month, but that's a stretch for many, including me! The two of us currently spend roughly $500 per month for food, which could easily double if we ate out more often.

Unlike Americans, most humans consume primarily dried grains, legumes, and vegetables which are far cheaper than meat and dairy. They also raise much of their own food including vegetables, chicken and other edible animals. In fact, meat is used more for flavoring or occasional treats than as a main course. This meat-as-flavoring diet is not only cheaper, but it's also more sustainable and healthier.

As grocery prices rise, you can either complain (which does no good) or eat less meat, dairy and processed foods (which does a lot of good). Vegetables are healthy, relatively inexpensive and you don't have to go fully vegan or vegetarian to increase your vegetable intake. Don't like anything green? Bummer Dude.

You can get your food cost down significantly by making wise choices. While lowering your food cost, you can also lower your cholesterol, blood pressure and weight. Biologists say that each of us replaces all of the cells in our bodies every 7-10 years. So you really are what you eat! I suspect that a few fast-food folks are like walking-talking cheeseburgers. No judgment here. Been there–done that.

As an off-gridder, you can certainly raise most of your food including meat and eggs, but it's not an easy life. When visiting our farm neighbors, we get to witness the amount of work and attention involved in raising domestic animals. We simply opt to purchase meat and dairy from the local farmers, while maintaining our property as a preserve for wildlife.

We don't hunt for meat but welcome friends and families that do. Currently there is an overpopulation of whitetail deer in our area, resulting in more deer ticks, deer diseases and deer damage to tree saplings. Oh deer! Since *Keystone Species* such as wolf and bear have been mostly eradicated, that means humans have to assume the role of deer population control. Are we doing a good job? Hmm, I dunno. I do know it's been a focus of debate for years!

## Gardening

For many, gardening is a passion and considered a must. The fact is that it takes time, diligence, and some cooperation from nature. This may be the healthiest way to go but it's not necessarily the easiest or cheapest. When you're busy working or building it can be a better use of your time to purchase fresh produce from the professionals (farmers and grocers).

**Did ya know,** Americans eat roughly one ton of food per year per person? Whoah! That's 2,000 pounds and doesn't include cans or packaging material. That's roughly equivalent to the weight of a classic Volkswagen Beetle, plus driver!

That being said, whatever you'd like to grow, just go for it! You'll find that some plants do better than others in your soil. Some things grow like weeds, others just wither or bolt too quickly. After a few years of trial and error, we found that the following vegetables thrive in our soil. They don't require insecticides and give us a good yield of food per hour of labor (Big Bang for the Buck).

**VEGGIES:** Swiss Chard, Kale, Squash, Cucumber, Tomatoes, Asparagus

**HERBS:** Oregano, Mint, Thyme, Basil, Epazote, Chives

Instead of growing only store-bought seeds, you can collect seeds from tomatoes, cucumbers, squash, pumpkin etc. In addition, you can grow from vegetable scraps. This technique works for onions, celery and root vegetables such as potatoes, carrots and turnips. It also works with onions and celery.

To dissuade deer, rabbits and bugs from eating all of your efforts, simply plant the stinkiest plants around more tasty vegetables. Anything that emits a strong odor will mask the milder aromas of fresh greens and vegetables. This includes: thyme, oregano, onions, garlic, chives, dill, basil, marigolds, rosemary and lavender. Mint and sweetgrass work too but can easily take over if not trimmed. Other odiferous deterrents include wood ash moth balls and even pee.

Does this odor fence really work? Well, the forest is full of rabbits and deer and we haven't lost much garden produce to the brown browsers. Chipmunks are undeterred by unusual smells and love to tunnel in our garden. However, we like 'em because they only eat a few of our veggies, while also eating mice and other wee invaders.

Soil is key to producing good healthy vegetables and there are ways to sweeten the mix. Good (and expensive) store-bought potting soil is one option, but you can make your own "special blend" using native dirt with one or more natural and readily-available additives: compost, wood ash, sand, etc. Home soil test kits measure acidity (pH) and levels of nitrogen, phosphorus, and potassium so you can fine-tune your blend. If you have poor soil and want to grow magnificent veggies, it's worth a few more dollars to send a soil sample to a laboratory for more detailed analyses, including trace mineral analysis. This helps uncover soil contaminants and deficiencies providing custom fertilizer prescription for your garden soil.

In the Fall before the first freeze, we bring our herbs and greens indoors. Many plants will continue to grow and can be used throughout the winter. This method works well for most herbs, kale, chard, arugula and other leafy greens. In addition, mushrooms can be grown indoors during winter months using purchased mushroom kits.

👉 Blue Oyster Mushrooms

Basil

Wintergreen

## Foraging

If you're not into greens or mushrooms, I'd say try foraging wild blackberries, blueberries or raspberries that ripen in late summer. There's lots to eat in the wild, but much of it is only ready to harvest for short periods. I'm not going too deep into foraging because there are much better books (and experts) on the topic. For more, check out the references at the end of this book.

## Universal Edibility Test

If you're gonna get into foraging, first do your research about each plant and any toxic look-a-likes. Then learn and practice the Universal Edibility Test (UET), a technique taught by the US Army as part of Survival Training. It involves testing the plant first on your skin, then bottom lip, then tasting and spitting out small then larger amounts. Each step involves several hours of waiting in-between to see if you develop an adverse reaction. The UET takes extra time, but should always be followed prior to chowing-down on any wild plant or mushroom.

## Lambsquarter
### (Wild Spinach)

Lambsquarter is a prolific green that we forage and enjoy frequently during the Spring and Summer. It tastes very similar to baby spinach, but provides substantially more nutrition. This *"weed"* has been pulled and discarded by unwitting humans for decades. To us, that's like discarding good food.

Lambsquarter seeds are beneath the soil throughout North America and show themselves once the soil is disturbed. It even pops-up in urban alleys and vacant lots. So when you disturb the soil, don't be surprised if this natural food shows up outta nowhere… like magic!

We harvest and consume Lambsquarter on a regular basis because it's delicious, nutritious and free. It's also an easy way to add a leafy-green super-food to your diet. Try it in scrambled eggs, spaghetti sauce or steamed with butter. You might be pleasantly surprised and wonder, *"Where have you been all my life"?!*

Ramps (wild leeks) are one of the first green plants to emerge in spring.

Wild Blueberries, Milkweed Flowers, and Goatsbeard Shoots

Purslanes

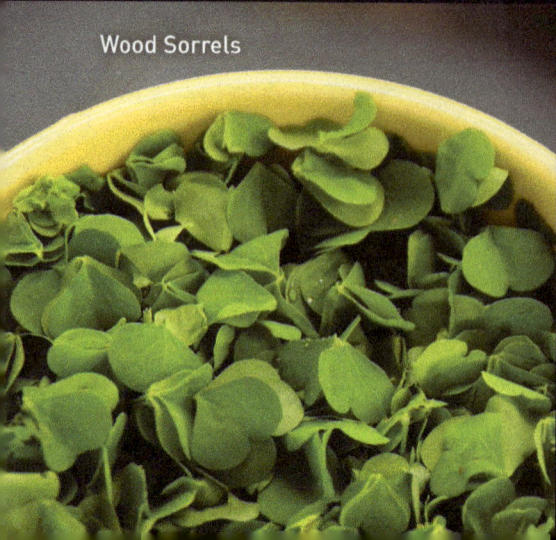
Wood Sorrels

## FORTH TO BASICS

Here are a few of our favorite foraged foods, when in season. There are more out there but we're still learning.

### Spring:

Maple Syrup
Ramps (Wild Leeks)
Fiddlehead Ferns
Morel Mushrooms
Dandelions
Cattail Roots
Nettles

### Summer:

Milkweed Pods and Flowers
Wild Blueberries
Wild Blackberries
Elderberries
Chicken-of-the-Woods Mushrooms
Lion's Mane Mushrooms
Goatsbeard Shoots
Wood Sorrels
Purslanes

### Fall:

Hazelnuts
White Oak Acorns
Hen of the Woods Mushrooms (Maitake)

## Shopping

Random, listless browsing can be expensive. Its a challenge to be frugal, but a well-planned shopping list and 30 minutes is all that's needed to stock-up on a week's worth of food. Some of my farmer neighbors shop for groceries only once a month. A little pre-planning and careful shopping go a long way towards reducing food costs, while keeping us healthy.

Blackberries

Ostrich Fern Fiddleheads

Nettles

Maple Syrup

Chicken-of-the-Woods Mushrooms

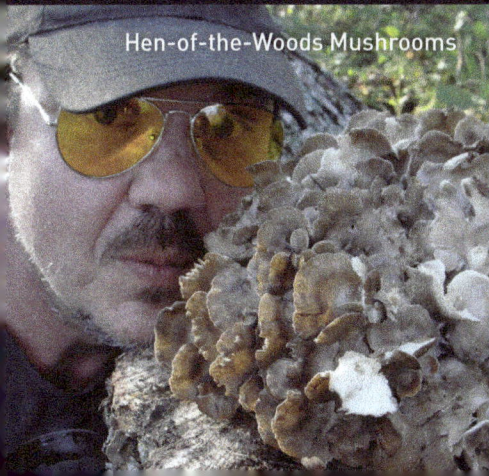

Hen-of-the-Woods Mushrooms

## BASIC KITCHENWARE KIT

- ○ Stainless Steel Pot with Strainer
- ○ Saucepan with Lid
- ○ Plates and Cutlery
- ○ Cutting Board
- ○ Spatula
- ○ Serving Spoon
- ○ Cast Iron Skillet

- ○ Can Opener
- ○ Measuring Cup with Pour Spout
- ○ Knife
- ○ Knife Sharpener
- ○ Peeler
- ○ Measuring Spoons

Photo: Bruce Christianson

## Preparation and Preservation

We usually get by with just a few basic kitchen utensils and don't need the latest greatest gadgets to prepare delicious and nutritious meals. No need to get all fancy! On the opposite page is a compilation of the kitchenware we use on a daily basis. This basic kit is relatively inexpensive and easy to pack for camping trips and outdoor picnics.

If you love cheffing, then by all means get some additional gadgets like a lemon juicer or meat grinder. One gadget we love is our rechargeable go-anywhere food processor. It helps to speed the prepping of fresh vegetables as soon as we return from shopping, harvesting or foraging. Quite a timesaver — it simplifies the tasks of fine chopping and grinding.

No use hiding fresh food items in the bottom of a refrigerator — we keep 'em on the countertop and use 'em 'til gone.

A little water in a glass will help keep asparagus and herbs fresh for days. Eggs don't need refrigeration if you consume them within a week or so. The same is true of tomatoes, onions, potatoes and other root vegetables. Each of these have developed their own defenses against bacteria and molds, but only for so long.

It's not how much food you buy or grow, it's how much you actually eat. Spoiled food is a waste of time, money and resources (and Yuck)! Refrigeration works quite well but it's an energy-hog and promotes *"out-of-sight- out-of-mind"* spoilage. Better to keep fresh food in plain view and prep ASAP. Yup, use it or lose it!

Here are some of our favorite tricks to extend the food's window of edibility at room temperature, without refrigeration:

- **Prep berries with sugar and/or lemon juice to deter mold**
- **Salt or marinate meats or fish prior to cooking**

## Here's to Your Health!

Lean into Vegan with a rechargeable food processor.

### V3 Liquid Salad:

**Cherry Tomatoes** (big hand full)

1 - **Cucumber** (big seeds removed)

1 - **Carrot** (peeled or not)

2 tbsp - **Vinegar** (and/or Lime Juice)

1-2 tsp - **Honey**

**Salt** (a pinch or so)

With a few more ingredients, you can have a V8.

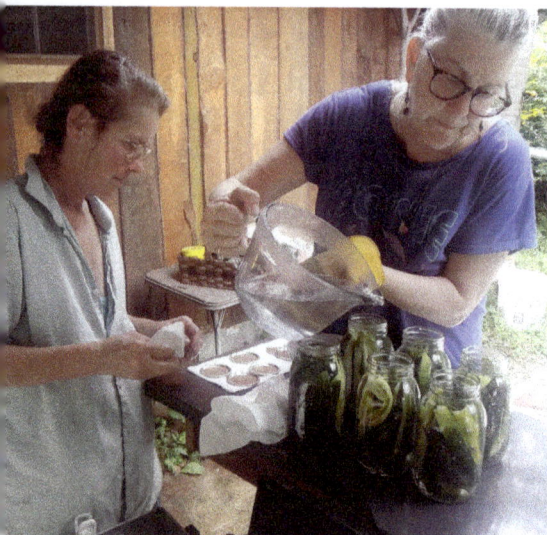

- Pickle cucumber and other veggies in a water-vinegar-sugar solution
- Smoke meats and fish with wood smoke
- Dry herbs, fruits, tomatoes, mushrooms, etc. above the wood stove or outside in the sun

Just like our grandparents did, we keep bread, crackers, and chips in a metal bread box to dissuade rogue rodents and mungy mold. Leftovers, fresh meats and dairy are kept on block ice in our super-insulated DIY icebox. **A block a week about does it!**

## Refrigeration

Refrigeration is one of the greatest inventions of modern man, keeping our food fresh for much longer than ever imagined. However, most good things have a downside and this is no exception. Leaking refrigerant gases as well as the large amount of energy needed to operate this modern convenience continue to contribute to our global warming dilemma.

As a cheaper solution to food preservation, we simply rely on a well-insulated icebox. Ice is not free and it typically requires electricity to produce, but for us, it's cheaper and easier than running a refrigerator 24/7. One block of ice can last up to a week during warm summer months. In winter, we make our own ice using muffin tins filled with water and placed outdoors. With winter's below-zero temperatures, the outside ice box can become a deep-freezer, so we move some foods and beverages inside to a cold corner of the house.

Our Amish neighbors have been using ice boxes for generations and still stockpile pond-harvested ice in sawdust for use in the summer. This may sound primitive, but it's the only kind of refrigeration people had up until the 20th century.

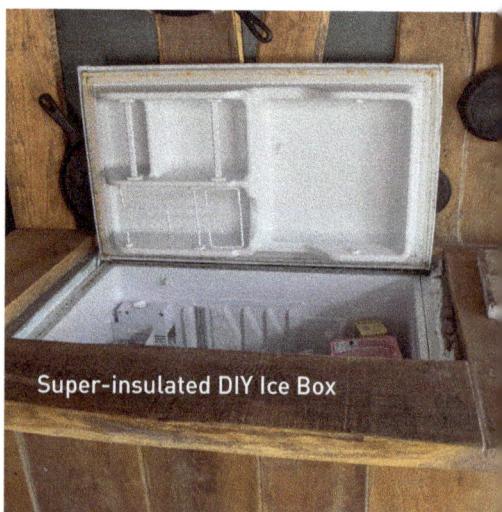
Super-insulated DIY Ice Box

# CLOTHING (PORTABLE SHELTER)

In warmer climates, you could survive indefinitely without clothes — just ask a Nudist!  Up here in Wisconsin, you'd be lucky to survive 3 hours outside in sub-zero January without clothing. Several Packer fans have tried!

## Layering

You may have heard the saying, *"There's no such thing as bad weather, just bad clothing."* If you shop well and layer properly, you can easily adjust your body temperature as needed. When winter temps get well below zero, we've gone as far as 6 layers! Most of the time, you can get by with just three layers: **Base, Mid and Outer.**

**Base Layer** — Your base layer can be very simple. A synthetic tee shirt and shorts could do the trick. If it's very cold you might opt for synthetic or wool-blend long johns (top and bottom or classic *Union Suit*).

**Mid Layer** — A mid-layer consists of all-purpose clothing that you can wear any time of year. Long sleeve shirts and light sweaters alongside pants of some kind are great for a mid-layer. These items aren't too thick, but they're just right to nestle over your base layer.

If it's a little colder, you might wear an insulating layer on top of your mid-layer. This wraps you in and keeps you from losing body heat. The insulating layer might include a synthetic pullover or wool sweater. The same goes for pants.

**Outer Layer** — The outer layer is also called a *"shell layer."* This consists of a waterproof jacket and pants. The purpose of the outer layer is to keep your interior layers safe from the wind, water and other elements.

## Natural Materials

We're not too picky about clothing but prefer natural materials (and used vs. new). Here are some natural materials that we use.

**Wool** — Wool comes from sheep, alpacas or llamas and is simply nature's finest fiber. It helps keep you warm and dry in winter, and cool and dry in summer. Each hair fiber is hollow, which makes it the perfect insulation for man (and beast).

**Silk** — Silk is another natural fiber brought to us by an amazing worm. Expensive but feels good, and has wicking properties. Snags easily so it works best as a base or mid layer. Silk undies? Why not? Nobody else needs to know!

**Cotton** — With winter campers the saying goes, *"cotton kills,"* and that's for one good reason: cotton tends to absorb and retain moisture. In cold weather this moisture can quickly lower your body temperature, sometimes resulting in hypothermia. Cotton is quite comfortable when dry but adding water or sweat makes it uncomfortable, even dangerous, in the cold. Best as a summer clothing choice.

**Hemp** — We hope to soon add clothing made from hemp-fiber fabric. It reportedly has great warming and cooling properties and grows like a weed. Oh yeah, it is weed but the stuff you don't wanna smoke! I'm unsure why it's not more widely available.

## Synthetic Materials

**Fleece** — Soft, warm and made from spun recycled plastic, fleece has excellent insulating and wicking abilities that outdoor athletes and winter enthusiasts love. It also emits micro-plastic particles in the dryer and can shrink. Best to air dry.

**Poly Blends** — Good for wicking moisture from skin but can become itchy after prolonged wearing. Lots of winter athletes wear hi-tech poly undies instead of cotton.

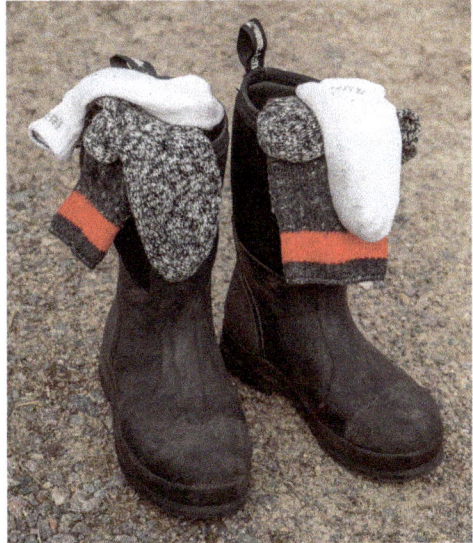

## Socks, Boots and Shoes

If you're going to splurge on anything, it should be on good wool-blend socks. Cold clammy feet are not my idea of fun. Double up on quality socks and rotate as needed. I've got several pairs and even triple up when venturing outside for extended periods in winter. Warm feet, warm bod.

If you live in areas prone to heavy rains and snowfall, you'll really appreciate a pair of waterproof summer and winter boots... In addition, a pair of comfortable slip-on shoes with good tread will save time when on the go. For comfy tootsies indoors, a pair of wool-lined slippers is just the ticket.

# SHELTER

If you've managed to save a nest egg of cash or equity, then you can build an energy-efficient shelter equipped with a propane heating system, private well, septic, and large solar panel array. This will provide maximum comfort and convenience while living off-grid. However, these conveniences are quite expensive and beyond the financial reach of many.

## Start Small, Add-On Later

While building our first shelter, we had to rough it for quite a while, sleeping first in a tent, then a camper trailer, then in a half-built cabin with a tarp as a temporary roof.

Some folks live in vans, campers, trailers, shacks, etc. while building their permanent structures. Some even keep the trailer on-site as a storage shed or guest house after construction is finished. Don't worry if someone calls you *"Trailer Trash."* Labelers gotta label. Just say, *"Thank you"* and *"You're welcome."*

At a bare minimum, you'll need a shelter that is dry and equipped with a fuel-burning stove. Our ancestors survived for centuries with no frills, just a simple structure with a rectangular foundation, doors, windows, wood stove and a bed. The "tiny home movement" seeks to fulfill just one need: to provide shelter from the elements, especially for nighttime sleeping. Shelter without heat is ok in some climates but not around here!

Veronica and I first built a small cabin on our land in which we lived full-time through two winters (one having a record-breaking snowfall of 100 inches!). The cost of living savings eventually allowed us to build a larger and more energy-efficient house. Our big shelter (house) opened up the cabin for friends, family and guests. Online booking sites, Airbnb and Hipcamp, have since allowed us to rent our cozy cabin to others seeking to get away and back to nature.

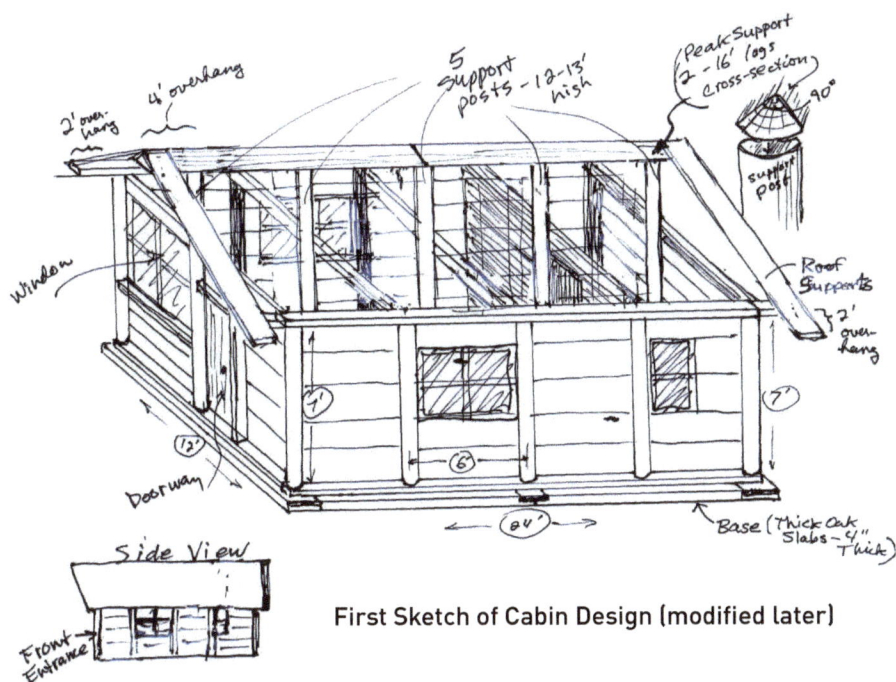

**First Sketch of Cabin Design (modified later)**

How large should your first shelter be? I'd say large enough for your needs but not so large that you're always feeding the fireplace in winter. 500-1,000 square feet is all that two people need for comfortable living.

For maximum versatility, you can place your furniture on wheels so your living space can easily convert to workspace, even a photo studio!

If your property has an existing structure, you may opt to take the renovation route. Do the math, estimate the total cost... then double it!

How you design and build your shelter is entirely up to you. I could detail exactly how we did it but that would take up another book! Instead, I'll provide some basic concepts and show you our process via photographs.

## Tap the Sun and Earth's Energy

The goal is to capture as much of the sun's energy in winter while avoiding much of it in summer. A shelter that allows direct sunlight to enter all year long is gonna become a hotbox during the dog-days of summer! A battery-powered fan does help but if you're gonna live without AC, good shelter design will keep you from losing your cool. By designing for both cold and hot weather, you'll avoid future discomfort.

It's a good idea to build into a south-facing hill to take advantage of the Earth's relatively constant 55-degree Fahrenheit temperature. Less heating is necessary in winter and less cooling required in summer. Of course, if there are no hills at your preferred site, then you can skip this design element... or do a lot of dirt diggin'!

## Thinking Outside the Box

Numerous books and websites are available that provide lots more detail about design (for free or cheap). If a simple box shelter seems too boring, there are many design options for adventurous builders. Here are a few other basic design options to choose from:

- A-Frame
- Geodesic Dome
- Tree House
- Modular
- Yurt
- Earthship (with shipping containers)

For design and layout, I just used pen and paper. But that's me. For more exact building plans there's free and fee software out there to avoid the substantial cost of hiring an architect:

**For free:**
- Homestyler
- Draft It
- Live Home 3D
- PlanningWiz

**For a fee:**
- SketchUp
- Floorplanner
- RoomSketcher
- TurboFloor Plan

**To utilize and control the Sun's energy to your best advantage, the following design elements are key:**

- Glass windows along the south side of the shelter
- 2 to 3-foot eaves over these south-facing windows
- Small windows on the east and west sides
- Few if any windows on north side
- Window awnings and/or light-blocking screens over west windows

Summer Sun

Winter Sun

## Lay a Firm Foundation

You don't want your shelter to sink or shift over time. With a good base foundation, this can be avoided. In remote areas, it can be trickier to obtain pre-mixed concrete. So if your driveway is just dirt and mud, nobody's gonna risk a stuck cement mixer at your location. No worries, you'll just have to get your back into it and make *homemade concrete!*

The simplest approach I've found is to place and level concrete blocks on native soil around the foundation perimeter. Then, mix homemade concrete and pour into the concrete block holes. The center of the building foundation can then be filled with gravel (if available) and/or covered with a thick PVC plastic sheet. If your building site tends to be wet or spongy, I recommend driving steel rods into the ground through the blocks before filling with concrete (see below).

An easier but more expensive option, is to buy Pier Block foundation corners with encased metal sleeves. These are made from high strength cast concrete. Six-foot metal spikes are driven through the sleeves and into the ground. This significantly increases the amount of weight supported. It's the preferred method used by the National Park Service for building walkways and shelters around wetlands.

### Homemade Concrete

**1 -** shovel Portland Cement

**4 -** shovels dry native sand (as clean as possible)

**3 -** shovels gravel

water

Mix in a tub or on an old sheet of plywood until fully incorporated but not too soupy.

## Focus on Roof

It's important to keep your shelter dry, season after season, year after year. Otherwise, you'll invite mold, mildew, fungus and insects that cause decay. Wooden homes with good roofs and siding can last for a hundred years or more. A damp leaky shelter might only last 10 years.

The best way to waterproof your shelter is to install a leak-proof roof with sufficient eaves to keep rainfall from hitting the outside walls and foundation. A two-three foot overhang will suffice. We chose metal roofing because of its durability and longevity. Metal roof panels are typically three feet wide and can be pre-cut to length then attached with hex-head roofing screws directly to the roof boards, plywood or OSB (Oriented Strand Board). For additional waterproofing and insulation, we covered the cabin roof boards with an ice & water shield underlayment, then 1-inch polystyrene-foam board insulation prior to installing the metal panels.

Other roofing options include standard shingles or even sod and dirt placed over a rubber or synthetic plastic sheet. Metal outperforms other options when it comes to damaging hail or wind-borne branches and the ribbed design has insulating qualities to reflect the sun during summertime.

## Seal, Insulate, Ventilate

How did 19th century people seal and insulate their shelters? Well, mostly they didn't. Homes were drafty, dusty, smokey, and chilly at times. With a large fireplace or metal stove, a little draftiness didn't matter and probably helped clear the air. Holes and cracks between logs or boards were patched with more wood, stuffed with rags and smeared with pine pitch or wax.

Here in the 21st century we have hi-tech caulk, sealants, spray foam and poly-foam board insulation. I recommend to use them liberally to seal your shelter. My purist friends have pointed out that these are petroleum-based chemicals and should be avoided. In my humble opinion (and I could be wrong) a small amount of petroleum used to increase the longevity of a permanent living space is petroleum well spent. Fuel use can be reduced significantly by using good sealants to fight the drafts. Sealants also prevent decay and keep bugs and mice out.

Do you really need to insulate your small shelter? Not necessarily, as long as it's tightly-sealed. Would you rather live in a well-sealed submarine or a well-insulated submarine? Insulation does help retain heat in the winter and cool in the summer, but it's spendy. I recommend insulating the roof but not the walls. Why? Because heat escapes up and out, but not so much sideways. Small cabins and log homes don't usually need wall insulation because thick wood acts as a barrier to heat loss (or gain).

Often, the fireplace or stove emits more heat than we can handle so we need to open a door or window. At these times, insulation is mostly irrelevant. The only insulation in our small cabin is the layer of 1" poly-foam board directly under the metal roof… and it's cozy as can be!

Ventilation is important to allow the inside to breathe and reduce the potential for mold, mildew and rot. Lack of proper ventilation can be an issue in some well-sealed buildings, but not so much in a small DIY shelter. If you leave a few tiny cracks or gaps around the doors and windows (and you will), then the space will breathe. The trick is to allow just enough ventilation to clear out any stove smoke and excessive humidity, but not so much that you feel a draft in winter.

**Fire Safety** In an emergency, these modern safety devices can really save your assets… and asses!

- Fire extinguishers
  — one for each door
- Combination CO/smoke detectors
  — one for each floor and room

Both are definitely needs if you burn fuel (any fuel). **Safety first 'cause sh*t happens!**

**Seal 'Er Up:** Modern Chinking with Foam and Caulk

**How much time did it take to build our cabin?** My best estimate is 1,000 hours over a 12-month period. Keep in mind that sealing and detailing often takes more time than the rough build. "Pretty" takes time!

# FUEL

You simply cannot live without fuel. We use it for cooking, transportation and occasional power tool usage. The fuel we utilize most is wood, followed by gasoline (for vehicles and generators) and propane (for outside barbeque grill).

## Wood

If you live in a forest, you can heat your shelter using only wood. We do not fell living trees, but rather utilize fallen trees and branches, which are everywhere here. A rule of thumb is that a five-acre plot of mature trees will provide more than enough fuel to heat a home, even through the harshest winters. That many trees will simply grow, die and shed limbs faster than you can burn it as fuel. Burning wood does emit greenhouse gases, but not as much as oil, gas or coal.

Some types of wood are better than others. Oak is the preferred fuel in our neighborwoods due to its high energy content and slow-burning characteristics. Softwoods like pine and cottonwood will burn just fine but they burn too quickly and often spit embers. Best to use the softwoods for starting the fire, then hardwoods like oak for a slower release of energy.

Properly seasoned (dried) wood, ready for splitting.

## How much fuel?

Our house/workshop is 800 square feet with a 200 square foot loft. Here's a rough estimate of our fuel requirements over the past 12 months:

**Wood** Three full cords. A cord is a stacked pile of split firewood measuring 4x4x8 ft.

**Gasoline** 40 gallons for Generators and ATV, 500 gallons for Transportation

**Propane** Six — 20-pound tanks

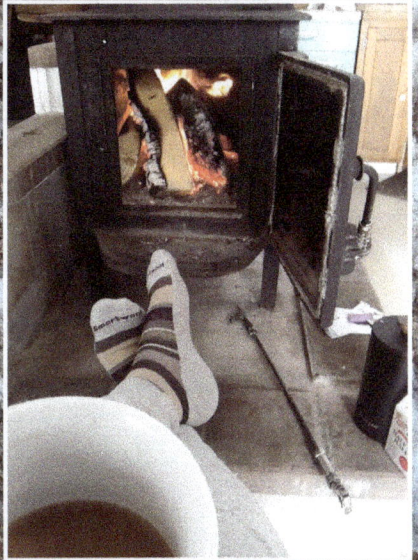

# FIREWOOD BASICS

I like to say, *Everything's easy once you've done it 100 times!* Fire making is one example and something that you WILL learn (eventually) if wood is your primary fuel. After lots of trial and error, here are some tips that may help save you time and unnecessarily hard labor!

## Cutting, Prepping and Chopping Wood

### Here's a few bits of wisdom of a thousand fires:

1. Cut fallen trees and large branches to 16" lengths — a good chainsaw is my tool of choice.

2. Stack or pile round 16" logs at the site where the tree was found or felled. No need to cover.

3. Prior to chopping, allow log rounds to season (aka, dry) for 6-12 months. Seasoned wood will turn grey. Radial checking (cracking) at the log ends signifies that it's time to split. Sections cut from standing dead trees may be split sooner.

4. Chop by hand using a "Tire Pie".

5. Stack chopped wood outside not too far and not too close to your shelter.

6. Bring chopped wood inside near stove to warm up and/or dry prior to burning.

## Tire Pie (Log Splitting)

Ok, this is my term which consists of placing logs into an old, discarded truck tire, then splitting the logs radially... just like cutting a pie! To split a log in half, first aim your splitting axe for the most prominent radial crack. Then continue striking in a straight line across the full diameter. This usually takes a few more whacks with big oak rounds. Once the log is split in two, the internal cohesion is relaxed and you can simply walk around and trim off smaller pieces of the pie.

This might seem like more work than using a hydraulic splitter, but I think it's easier and faster because you don't have to chase split pieces and re-stack every time you split! Anybody wanna race?

## Building a Fire
### (like a Norwegian)

It took me years to learn how to make a fire correctly and efficiently. That eureka moment came from the Norwegians, who have for centuries depended on only wood as fuel. They simply build their fires with large logs underneath and kindling on top, rather than vice versa.

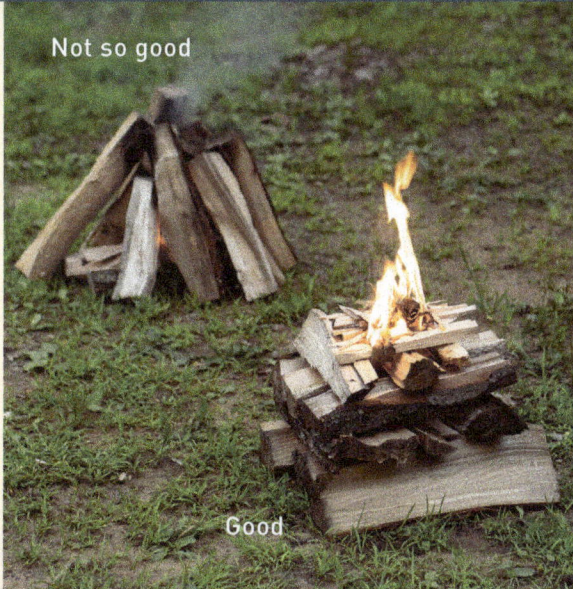

Not so good

Good

## How Much Wood?

To estimate the amount of wood needed annually for heating and cooking needs, a good rule of thumb is as follows:

**Two to three cords of wood** are required to heat a well-built, well-sealed 1,000 square foot shelter. If your shelter is under construction or noticeably drafty, then better get four cords! If you live in warmer climates, two might do.

*What is a cord of wood? See the next page.*

Wood Dryer Teepee

## What's a Cord?

It's an age-old standard of measurement that is simply a stacked pile of split firewood measuring 4-feet high, 4-feet wide, and 8-feet long. Each piece of firewood is roughly 16" long to fit into most stoves and fireplaces; therefore, a stacked cord (aka "Full Cord") has three rows of stacked "Face Cords".

Yup, a cord is a big pile o' wood! Firewood is often sold in a variety of measures, from truck-loads to bundles. To help keep things straight (and avoid the con) here are some relatively rough but useful conversions.

### 1 Full Cord

= 3 Face Cords
= 128 cubic feet
≈ 3500-5000 pounds (dry oak)
≈ 6000+ pounds (green oak)
≈ 2 large trees (18" diameter)
≈ 2-3 (1/2-Ton) pickup truck
   or trailer loads
≈ 3 pallets (wrapped)
≈ 144 gas-station bundles

(≈ rough equivalent)

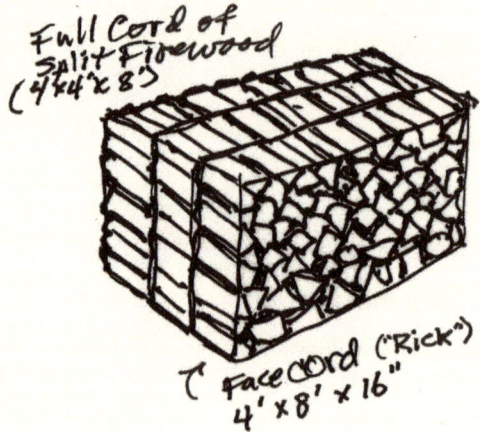

Full Cord of Split Firewood (4'x4'x8')

1 Face Cord ("Rick") 4' x 8' x 16"

If you don't have sufficient access to wood, there are other options including wood pellets, corn, fuel oil or propane. Wood pellets or corn require a special type of furnace and may or may not be cheaper than propane depending on where you live. Fuel oil is cheaper than propane, but it's dirty, smelly, messy and not worth the effort (in my opinion).

### Propane

Propane, or Liquid Petroleum (LP) Gas, is a slightly heavier version of natural gas that's specifically formulated for tank storage and distribution. It's currently more than double the cost of natural gas and is the most-used fuel in rural homes.

If you're gonna install a whole-house propane heater, I'd recommend a professionally installed system. DIY only when you really know what you're doing! Improperly installed propane heaters can lead to carbon monoxide poisoning which is sometimes fatal. Although technology has improved greatly as far as burners and shutoff valves go, there's still a risk of something going wrong. It's a good idea to have a small backup propane heater available to get you through the coldest days of winter. We've only used our unvented backup propane heater once in five years. The wood stove keeps us plenty warm.

### Gasoline

In addition to using gasoline (gas) for transportation to/from town, we use it to fuel our four-wheel-drive ATV, chainsaw and electric generator. This gas usage is small compared to vehicle usage. You can cut and haul a lot of firewood with a 4-wheeler and five gallons o' gas! You can also fuel a (quick -n- dirty) electric generator to produce AC electricity for $1 to $3 an hour.

A gas-powered generator will run almost any electric power tool but, due to the noise and exhaust, we operate them infrequently. Now that we have a solar power system installed, the gas-powered generator is operated only as needed, and it ain't needed very much these days.

### Seasonal Fuel

Since our wood stove is burning wood all day, every day in the winter, this is our source of cooking heat for five-six months per year. During the warmer months, we don't need (or want) to heat up the house. Years ago, before air-conditioning, kitchen cook stoves were

often moved outside to the porch during summer. This is what we do. If you can't take the heat… move the kitchen!

We typically purchase a 20-gallon LP tank every two months for cooking outside during warm weather.

In addition to cooking food, both the wood stove and the propane grill are essential for heating water as needed… for making coffee, washing dishes and even bathing (but nothing fancy).

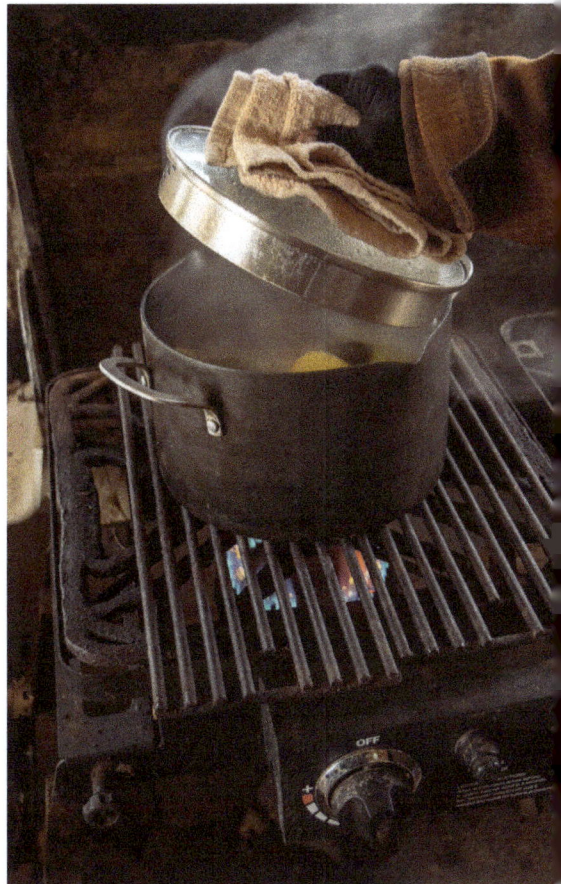

# SANITATION

You might ask whether sanitation is a "need." You can certainly live with messy surroundings, but if you don't deal with wastes on a daily basis, you'll regret it. How will you regret it? Think flies, smells, mice, etc. In addition to dealing with wastes, you simply need to bathe and wash clothes and dishes. Is sanitation optional? Nope. Is it a need? Yup.

## Septic System

This is one area where the good ole days weren't all that good. Disease and bad stink were pretty common, especially in big cities. It's still common in poverty-stricken areas. Us country folk have learned that pee/poo control cannot be ignored or you'll invite odor, flies and potential sickness.

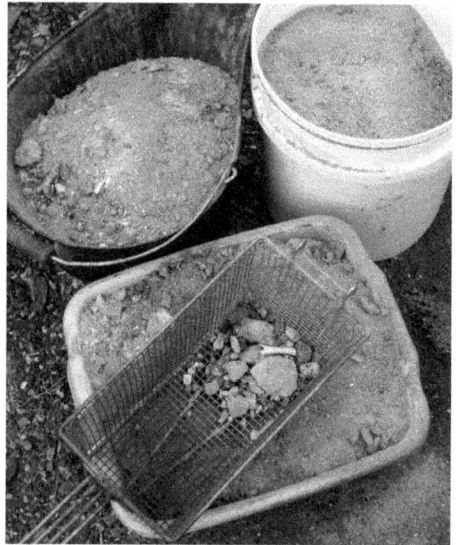

The legendary outhouse (with pit) is one of the simplest types of bathroom and has been a popular place of business for centuries. This is what we utilize at our property. You definitely have to check with local regulations before installing one. In many rural counties, they are legal as long as the bottom of the pit is at least two feet above groundwater. This is the first building we constructed on our property and we paid a small fee to have an inspector pre-approve the outhouse location.

To reduce outhouse odor we simply *"Flush with Ash."* Actually, we alternate between wood ash and wood chips to cover each day's business. This simple practice helps keep flies and stink to a minimum. Wood ash neutralizes acid and is a natural deodorizer. By promoting bacterial activity through layering of these materials, it's amazing how fast the volume of material is reduced. For two people, a well-built (and maintained) outhouse can last for 5+ years. After that, the structure can be moved to a new pit. Of course, the old pit needs to be covered and compacted... or you might take an unexpected and unpleasant trip!. If you'd rather not move the outhouse, a local

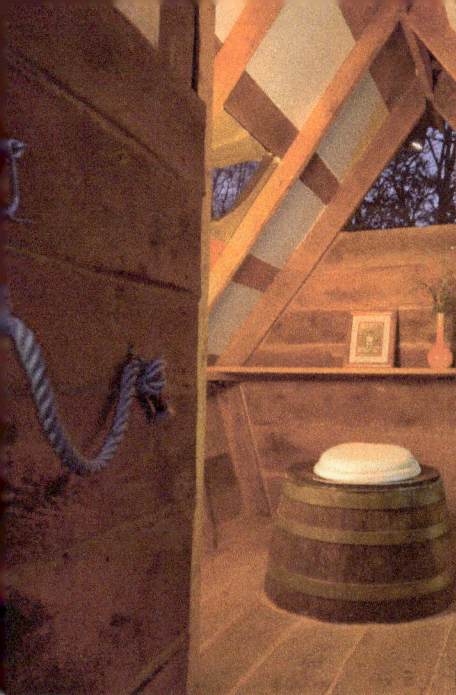

Photo: Bruce Christianson

## Flush with ash!

 Wood ash buckets with fry basket for removing metal and other debris.

**The following materials can also be periodically added to reduce odor and promote bio decomposition:**

- ○ Peat moss
- ○ Straw
- ○ Sawdust
- ○ Cooked cabbage

**DO NOT add the following:**

- ⊘ Hot ashes
- ⊘ Meat scraps
- ⊘ Oil/grease
- ⊘ Insecticides
- ⊘ Bleach! ...*Combining bleach with acidic urine creates more toxic gas than you can possibly produce yourself!*

Loo Build

septic service may be able to pump the contents to a truck-mounted tank. This will extend the outhouse's useful life. Some people dig up old outhouse pits for garden compost but we don't. That's too much *"Doody Duty"!* If you decide to mine the old outhouse pit for fertilizer, I'd let it decay for five years so all nasty components are fully broken down.

Other off-grid toilet options include:
- **Composting Toilet**
- **Incinerator Toilet**
- **"Porta-Potty"**
- **"Business Bucket"**
- **"Nature Walk"**

Most are DIY solutions, but the Porta-Potty, whether rented or purchased,

usually needs to be emptied and serviced by a reputable septic service company.

> **Q: Does a bear sh*t in the woods?**
> **A:** Yes but rarely in the same place!

In emergencies, it's okay to go outside, provided that you don't have spectators (that's rude) and you're careful to bury it (that's gnarly). Any uncovered poo will stink to high heaven and draw flies and possibly disease. After all, *"You don't poop where you eat!"*

### Food Waste and Trash Control

When it comes to wild critters, I tell folks, *"If they find a snack, they'll be back."* This is precisely why you don't want trash, especially food waste, outside near your

**Did ya know,** each American on average uses 140 rolls of toilet paper per year? That's a whole lotta wipin' goin' on! In the old days, they used other methods — everything from corn cobs to washable mittens... Just say "Whoa!"! These days, we opt for a TP brand made of recycled paper. This stuff breaks down quite nicely in our outhouse pit and isn't too expensive. Who Gives a Crap? We do!

shelter. If you live in the wild like we do, food scraps (especially meat scraps) can lure anything from mice to bears and everything in-between.

After hosting our 2014 wedding reception, we were visited (loudly) by raccoons each night for weeks! No bone or used napkin was left unturned. It's amazing how one barbecue can make your yard a furry scavenger's hunting grounds. For the rest of the summer, the raccoons must have considered us as *"The Land of Tasty Snacks"*. We either burn meat scraps in the wood fire or bury it well away from camp.

Ever since we have established a *"No-snack-for-you"* policy, we infrequently encounter wild animals, except for the occasional chipmunk, rabbit, squirrel or frog.

We know larger animals are out there cause we've seen 'em on the *"critter cam"* and see their footprints in fresh mud and snow. In fact, we hear coyotes at night but rarely see them. They don't bother us 'cause

there's nothing to eat and it smells like humans… and they avoid humans (fortunately)… but we like them!

**Chip!**
If they find a snack, they'll be back!

## Bathing

For years, our routine included a daily shower. Living off-grid makes this modern luxury impractical but not impossible. Not having a daily shower may seem like a deal-breaker for some, but you have to ask yourself, *"how clean do you need to be?"* Lots of skin problems stem from over-showering. Not that you want to be a walking stench-fest, but you can get by with much less bathing than you might think. Not that long ago in America, a weekly bath or shower was all that was needed.

The frequency of washing depends on your own comfort zone. Nobody wants rashy skin, so a weekly bath of any kind is better than a monthly or seasonal bath! Whoa.

Our most common method in winter is a simple PTA (pits, tits and ass) bath. All you need is warm water and a washcloth. Heads before tails! Other methods we use include:

- **Wet Wipes** (best invention since TP!)
- **Shower bag** (outside except for winter…Brrr!)
- **Battery-powered shower head with pump**
- **Hillbilly shower** (Dang good!)
- **Sauna** (not just for Swedes anymore!)

A sauna is a necessity for some who live in Nordic Europe and Canada but not as much here in the Midwest. After our cabin was finished, we built a sauna (with free pallets and lumber). We've also found that it takes a fair amount of firewood, time and effort to get it warmed-up above 90-degrees Fahrenheit. For two people, that's not something we want to do every day. However, when we have family and friends over who share all the work, then it's well worth it. Sauna should be a sober zone, and I have a burn scar to prove my point!

Sauna Build

Photo: Bruce Christianson

### Laundering

…clothes only! Similar to washing dishes, you can use the same heated water to wash clothes in a tub. We do this on occasion using simple laundry soap (no bleach or mystery fragrances). Drying is accomplished the old-fashioned way, on a clothesline. Hey, it works like a breeze!

A self-serve coin-operated laundromat is a good option if there's one within a reasonable distance. We are fortunate to have one six miles away. Typically, we make this journey once a month, and although it isn't free, it's way more convenient than hand-washing and drying everything.

### Doin' Dishes

For washing dishes, we typically use rainwater in summer and snow in winter. Rainwater can be used to rinse dishes but only if it's from a recent rain. Rainwater sitting in a barrel or tub can get skanky. Any of this water can be heated on the wood stove or propane grill to boil off contaminants. We tend to use cool water for washing and hot water for rinsing.

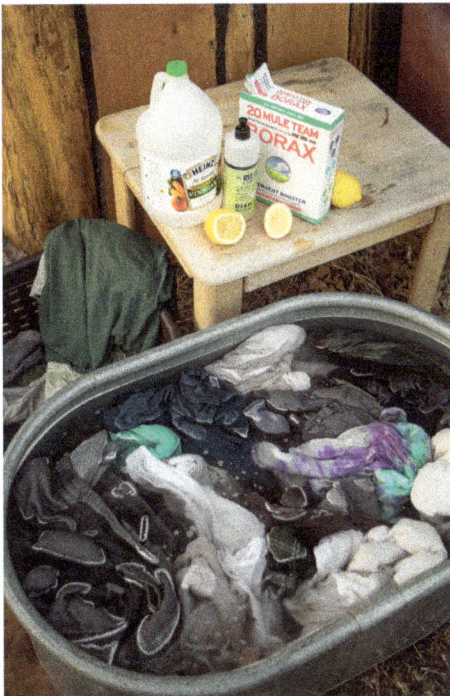

We typically **clean cast iron pans** with 1 Tbsp coarse salt and a cloth, followed by a wipe with oily cloth. Water + Iron = Rust, so standing water will result in rust-flavored food and extra work later.

## NATURAL CLEANING PRODUCTS

Many cleaning products contain chemicals you've never heard of and probably don't want to. Some people are irritated by these chemicals, especially the fragrances. **Did ya know,** manufacturers are not required to list the components of the fragrances for proprietary reasons? We opt to purchase simple fragrance-free laundry soap or just **make our own cleaning products** from tried-and-true components.

### White Vinegar

When mixed with water, this edible acid makes a great overall cleaner for most surfaces. Try a quarter-cup of vinegar per gallon of water. White vinegar cuts grease, inhibits mold, kills bacteria and freshens the air.

### Citric Juice

(lemons, limes, and oranges, oh my!)

These are also edible acids that help lift stains and fight bacteria.

### Borax

Borax is a naturally occurring alkaline mineral that used to be found in many processed foods until that unhealthy practice was outlawed. I wouldn't eat it, but it works great in small amounts as a laundry booster. Discovered 4,000 years ago, it cleans and deodorizes.

### Baking Soda

(aka sodium bicarbonate)

This substance has been used for centuries to neutralize acid (that means heartburn relief, too). It also has many other uses including dissolving grease and dirt, as well as deodorizing. Can also be used for scouring surfaces and pans.

### Salt

Salt, *"it's not just for seasoning."* Coarse salt is great for scouring cast iron cookware. It also acts as an ant deterrent.

### DIY All-purpose Cleaning Solution

2 ½ cups water

3 T white vinegar

½ tsp liquid soap

Photo: Bruce Christianson

# FINDING BALANCE

### Sleep and Rest

Keep in mind that sleep and rest are not the same thing. Sleep is not always restful and rest is not always during sleep. A 20-minute nap, or meditation session can be more restful than three hours of restless sleep. During our building phase, Veronica and I often overworked ourselves to exhaustion. We made progress, but the next two days we were too sore to do anything but complain. Not a very wise use of our time! These days, we operate under a more realistic and sustainable work/rest routine. Remember, slow and steady wins the race!

### Balance

**I believe that balance is a key component to individual success, happiness and contentment.**

Simply stated, needs and wants should be balanced with costs and impacts. Whenever I DIY, I attempt to maximize benefits (function, form, safety and fun) while simultaneously minimizing costs (money, time, effort and impacts). Of course, it's always preferable that benefits outweigh costs.

**Built with Balance**

*"Work 'til you're sore,
rest 'til you're bored."* — Me

# WANTS OR NEEDS?
## YOU DECIDE

### What else do you need?

In this chapter, we'll delve into the wants that you could probably live without, but still want or need because they provide income, comfort, convenience and even enjoyment. These include things like tools, electric power, automobiles, phones, computers, etc.

# BEYOND THE BASICS

In Chapter 2 we discussed our basic human survival needs. Theoretically, if you can fulfill these basic needs you can subsist just about anywhere. Might have to trade goods with neighbors and borrow some tools, but otherwise, you're pretty much covered. See the **Basic Model of Survival** (illustration below).

In Chapter 3 we'll explore more needs and wants that help make our lives easier. We simply took the basic model and added the following modern innovations:

○ Modern tools

○ 400-watt solar system

○ Batteries for energy storage (2 large, 1 medium, 6 small)

○ Satellite dish Wi-Fi service

○ Cell phones

○ Laptop computer

○ Gas-powered 4x4 truck

○ Gas-powered ATV (All Terrain Vehicle)

○ Backup gas-powered electric generator

○ Food and ice from the store

# TOOLS

You can and should borrow tools whenever possible to avoid unnecessary costs and impacts. No matter how you access them (buy or borrow but please don't steal) you're simply gonna need tools before you can build anything.

During roughly 3,000 hours of building our cabin, outhouse and house, I've found that most carpentry can be accomplished with only a few simple hand tools. It's often easier to grab a hand tool than fire up a generator to run a power tool. The hand tool option is often faster, quieter, more portable… and less smokey!

## BASIC HAND TOOLS

**Top left:**
- Crowbar
- Speed Square
- Bits for Screwdriver
- 3-lb Mini Sledge (The Persuader)
- Pliers
- Saw
- Utility Knife
- Tape Measure
- Crescent Wrench
- Screwdriver
- 5-in-1 Painter's Tool
- Hammer
- Vice Grips
- Pencil
- Chainsaw Scrench
- Safety Glasses

Photo: Bruce Christianson

Early in our off-grid adventure, we realized that a few key labor-saving devices could really streamline our efforts. Here are a few of our favorites, including a 2002 4x4 ATV with trailer, which helps us move firewood and drag logs.

## ELECTRIC TOOLS

- Fan (my second best friend on a hot day)
- Vacuum
- Water Transfer Pump
- Radio
- Power Drill
- Batteries and Charger

## SNOW REMOVAL TOOLS

If you live in northern climates as we do, then you'll need at least a snow shovel or two to dig out after a heavy snowstorm. Instead of buying a snowblower or snowplow, we typically hire a neighbor to plow us out. A record breaking winter gave us a 4-foot snowfall that left us snowbound for six days! We had enough food and water so it wasn't so bad... even a little fun!

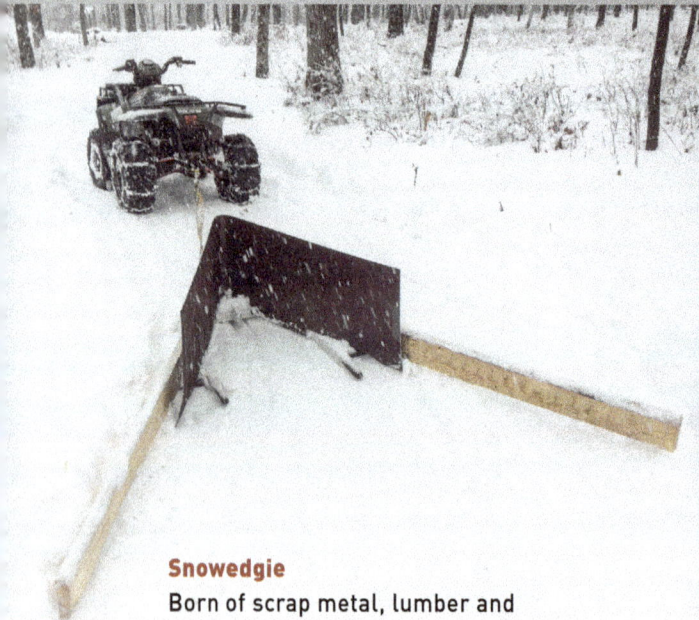

**Snowedgie**
Born of scrap metal, lumber and necessity after back-to-back blizzards.

## LABOR-SAVING
## DEVICES (clockwise)

○ 4x4 ATV
○ Trailer
○ Sled
○ Chainsaw
○ Shovel
○ Rake
○ Steel Pry Bar (Spud)
○ Logging Chain
○ Sawhorse with
　Foot-Operated Vice
○ Garden Cart
○ 8-lb Splitting Maul
○ Old Truck Tire

Small solar panel for two pendant lights

Four 100-watt solar panels

Storage batteries

Solar Roller — portable power

# OFF-GRID ELECTRIC POWER

## Solar Power
### (Slow and Clean)

Right after we finished the roof of our home, we installed a modest 400-watt solar system. This is what's considered a *"Starter Kit"* for off-grid living and includes:

- Four 100-watt panels
- One solar controller box
- Two 100-Ah AGM lead-acid batteries
- One 1200-watt power inverter

The solar controller keeps the batteries from overcharging, while the power inverter converts the batteries' 12-volt DC energy to standard 110-volt AC energy.

Our solar system costed roughly $1,000 (2018 prices) and now delivers most of the power we need to charge up tools, run the computer, TV and Wi-Fi modem. This setup is great for running electronics but it's not really powerful enough to run things with motors (air conditioners, refrigerators) or heating elements (electric space heaters, water heaters, microwaves). We could install a much larger system to run these devices but that's a lot of $$ for only slightly more convenience.

Look at cheaper options first. For instance, an icebox or a small propane-powered refrigerator is cheaper than a full-time, full-size electric fridge.

Much larger battery packs are available for on-grid homes as temporary back-up power, mainly to keep the refrigerator going. They can be used for off-grid homes but require a much larger solar panel array. Yes they are nice... and expensive! We'll stick to cheap-n-portable for our needs.

Here are a few insights to help simplify the solar installation process.

1. Mount panels on roof or roof extensions. Yard-mounted solar arrays requires longer (less efficient) wiring.

2. Mounts need to be strong enough for 80-mph wind gusts (and not wiggly).

3. It's ok to use treated wood to mount panels to roof. Metal mounts may require grounding.

4. Position solar panels at approximately 45 degrees with respect to the horizon, facing south toward the sun (northern hemisphere). You can make the mount adjustable for optimum seasonal sun-ray collection, but if fixed, better to optimize for winter when the sun is low and snow may pile-up on panels.

5. **Monocrystalline** and **Polycrystalline** type solar panels work well, the first being more efficient and expensive. Small and cheap portable solar panels of the **Amorphous** solar type are significantly less efficient.

6. Solar controllers usually come in one of two types: MPPT (maximum power point tracking) and PWM (pulse width modulation). The first is more efficient but more expensive. We get by with a cheaper PWM controller.

7. Get a good power inverter. A 1200-watt inverter works for our needs. It

converts the 12 volt DC energy stored in the main battery bank to 112-volt AC power.

8. If you don't want to run wires all over, just bring wires to a central charging station. Our panels come with 15-ft. wires so the charging station is not far from the outside panels. Only one hole through the roof vent was necessary!

9. It was way easier to install than we thought. The plugs are all matched, making cross-wiring relatively impossible. Once we plugged it in, it all worked!

10. One sunny day is equivalent to several (4-6) cloudy days when it comes to charging batteries.

11. There are a few (short) days in the winter when we run outta sun and then battery power.

### Simple Solar Lighting

I know, candlelight is awesome but please for safety sake, forget about indoor candles and oil lamps! Why? 'Cause burned shelters suck... and *Solar Rules!*

We simply utilize two LED light bulbs screwed into old AC lamps, which are plugged into the 1,200 watt solar inverter. These two bulbs each draw 13 watts and emit a bright warm hue equivalent to a 60 watt incandescent bulb. Our other solar lights consist of 8"x10" solar panels wired through the wall, each to two hanging pendant lamps inside. We also charge small outdoor solar patio lights, then bring 'em in for accent lighting (or as flashlights).

In addition, rechargeable flashlights and headlamps can not only light your way but can be aimed at the ceiling or into a lampshade for just the right ambiance.

Personally, I like the warm LED lights because they feel cozier and more candle-like than cold, blue daylight bulbs. A web search of "Warm Solar Lights" will reveal the many options. Some like the day-lights for reading or detail work. Either way, research the ratings, units sold and comments to weed out throwaway brands. Solar lights don't last forever, but longer than incandescent bulbs... and they don't start fires like other options!

1. **Solar lighting kit** that includes one solar panel and two LED pendant lights, each with rechargeable battery. It also comes with a 15-foot power cords and a remote to control the light intensity and color temperature (warm or white).

2. **Waterproof solar spotlight** with internal battery. Can be aimed into a lampshade for accent light.

3. **Camping lantern** with rechargeable 6-volt battery cartridge.

4. **Personal headlamps** each with three rechargeable AAA-batteries. Best to find 'em before the sun goes down!

5. **Portable spotlight** with rechargeable 20-volt battery. Can be aimed at the ceiling for a soft lighting effect.

## Know Your Load

Before you expect your solar system to do all the heavy lifting, consider this fact: Any electrical device with a motor or heating or cooling elements will require a lot more energy than simple lighting and communication devices. To demonstrate this, consider the following maximum energy loads, in watts, for common household devices.

Typical peak energy demands of modern devices (W=Watts)

**Power-able with 400 W of Solar Panels and 1000 W Inverter:** ⚡

LED Lamp 13 W
WiFi Router 20 W
20V Battery Charger 50 W
CPAP Machine 50 W
Laptop Computer 100 W
Television 100 W
Dehumidifier 300 W

**Requires gas-powered generator -or- way mo' Solar:** ⚡⚡⚡⚡

Coffee-maker 1000 W
Microwave 1000 W
Small Window AC 1500 W
Refrigerator 2000 W
Circular Saw 3500 W
Water Pump 4000 W
Water Heater 5000 W

## CUP-O-SUN

Our new favorite method of powering small to medium electronic devices is to borrow a "Cup-o-Sun" — "Huh?" — It's simply any lithium-ion battery charged by the Sun via solar panels.

Most of our battery-powered tools run on 20-volt rechargeable lithium-ion batteries. These are re-charged daily or weekly, depending on needs. Now that we've purchased three Cups-o-Sun, we can simultaneously run the drill and vacuum cleaner while listening to music on the radio! We charge 'em by plugging into our solar system's 1200-watt inverter. In a pinch, they can be charged wherever and whenever AC power is available (hotel rooms, friend's houses, solar roller, etc.).

There are larger and more powerful versions of Cup-o-Sun with built-in inverters, and their prices seem to be coming down. Some call them "solar generators" but are more accurately described as "solar storage vessels". For roughly $200 we purchased a nice unit that provides 24 amp-hours of AC energy (288 watt-hours). Whenever we need a little juice to power a TV, computer, wifi router or small fan, this unit comes in very handy. It can run each (but not all) of these items for several hours.

Think of the Cup-o-Sun as a point-of-use energy source. Just take it where ya need it. Wanna watch the football game outdoors? You grab the TV and antenna, I'll grab a Cup-o-Sun!...and the beer cooler.

Photo: Bruce Christianson

## Generator Power
### (Quick and Dirty)

If you need high power for an hour or so... just pull the cord! For some serious wattage, you can access quick (& dirty) 112 volt AC power with a gas-powered generator.

We own two. One is a 4,000-watt generator for occasional power tool use and the other a 2,000-watt inverter-generator for electronics. We used them frequently during construction but nowadays they mostly sit idle. We now have ample solar power for our daily needs and don't need to fire up the big power tools very often.

One of the biggest downsides to gas-powered electric generators (besides noise) is the exhaust fumes. They warn you not to operate inside or near an open door or window because of the carbon monoxide and unburned hydrocarbons. We ignored this warning once by placing the generator too close to an open window. After a few minutes, we started feeling nauseated, then our carbon monoxide detector started blaring. Yikes!

# TRANSPORTATION

Ok, I happen to know several fine folks who live and thrive without owning an automobile. From inner-city folks to Amish farmers, not everyone needs an automobile for transportation. However, most folks are not ready, willing or able to transition to the bus, electric car or horse and buggy. In that case, you can still use your car or truck wisely by minimizing frivolous trips. What's frivolous is up to you, but we try to limit trips to town to once per week.

Since we live in "The Land of Mud and Snow," our vehicle of choice is a 20-year old 4x4 pickup truck with a topper. Mileage is lousy, but it beats getting stuck in your own driveway. As gas prices rise, we just trim our travels. Above all, we try not to spend $10 on gas in order to save $10 on a purchase. Veronica and I each used to spend roughly 2 hours per day commuting to and from work. Some like driving and find it relaxing, some don't. We're just glad we don't have to drive nearly as much these days (Sigh).

# COMMUNICATIONS

## Phone
### (Smart or Dumb)

My generation grew up with the rotary dial telephone, but for the past decade my wife and I have been 100% cellular. No land lines. We have definitely saved money but sometimes poor coverage makes it difficult to do business and maintain friendships. A cell phone booster is on our wish-list but we're not sure if it'll work. If there's absolutely no signal, a booster won't help.

## Personal Computer

Personal computers have been around for only 40 years but have already revolutionized the way we work, play, communicate and live. It's become an indispensable tool when it comes to problem solving and productivity. Your computer can either be the most important time-saving tool in your toolbox…or you can be the tool.

Millions of people use their computers for communication and entertainment but

its greatest gift is how it gives us access to accumulated human knowledge from all over the globe. It's a portal to the greatest library known to humankind, right at your fingertips… The *"Earth Public Library"!* With this revolutionary tool, you can dip deep into the well of human knowledge. This well is somewhat murky at the top but there's crystal clear artesian knowledge down below.

If you spend 6-8 hours a day on YouTube, Twitter, Facebook, Instagram, Netflix or other on-online-entertainment, that's not necessarily wasted time. Lots of folks work on these platforms. That being said, we all need entertainment and social interaction, but make sure there's time left to take care of other business…like making ends meet!

For off-grid living a laptop rules — their new batteries can go all day on one charge. We charge ours with solar energy. I do miss my old iMac with 21-inch screen but it used a lot of juice… and ultimately crashed and burned! Luckily I had backups so not all was lost. Here's our new off-grid computer system which I used to write this book:

- 1 laptop (PowerMac)
- 3 external hard drives
- 1 printer

Mac or PC? Mac is more expensive but has many advantages, especially for folks in the visual arts. PC works just fine for most. Just do your research and balance needs (and wants) with costs!

## Wi-Fi

If you live in the *boonies* like we do, getting a Wi-Fi signal can only be accomplished by either setting up a hot-spot with your smartphone or by installing a satellite dish with modem. Either way, you have to pay a monthly fee for the service. If you work from home, this is definitely a need. Without Wi-Fi in our shelter, this book would still be pile of hand-written notes!

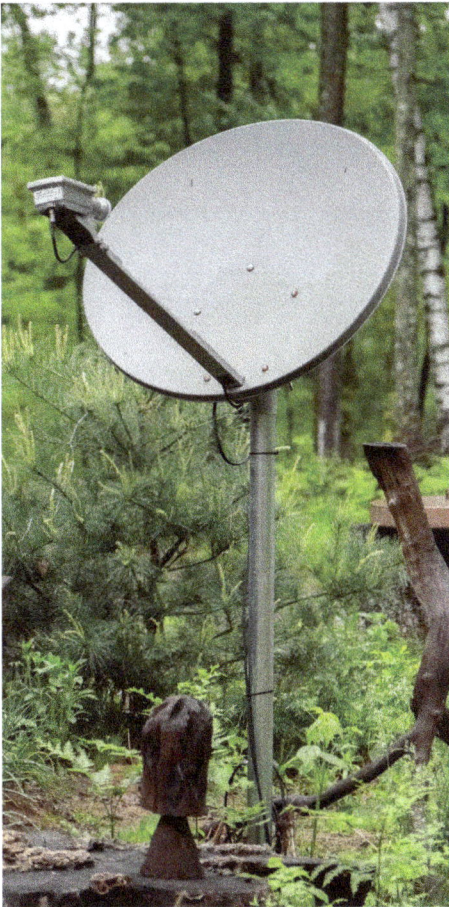

# MEDICAL CARE

Is medical care a need? It most definitely IS when you become sick or injured. Other times we just think of it as a big money pit. I can tell you that my wife and I had no medical insurance for the first decade of the 21st Century because we worked as sole-proprietors and could not earn enough income to keep up with rising premiums. Health care costs are still a major concern for most people.

In the old days, most health care was given at home by family members… or, if you were lucky, a good doctor would make a house-call. Either way, there was often nothing they could do but make you stay in bed. Some old-school remedies even made things worse. Ever hear of the practice of blood-letting? Whoa.

These days, we have great doctors, nurses and even volunteers who are ready to treat our every ailment. First, we should give these heroes a standing ovation for their front line fight against the recent pandemic. Second, we should realize that not every ache, scrape or sneeze requires an emergency room visit. We keep a couple of home remedy books around and have even communicated with nurses and doctors via the internet to first check whether a special trip to the doctor is warranted.

With modern tech, there are more things you can do to effectively heal yourself without breaking the bank, or even leaving the bed!

Most of the time, our medical care is DIY. A good standard first aid kit with a bottle of hydrogen peroxide is all you needs for minor cuts, scrapes and burns. DIYers often go through more bandages than average, so extra boxes (strategically stashed), will come in handy for inevitable boo-boos.

Basic first aid kit, with extra bandages and hydrogen peroxide.

# INCOME

*"Where your talents and the world's needs cross, there lies your vocation."*
— Aristotle

I've found that it's easier not to spend a dollar than it is to make a dollar. That said, you still have to make a dollar to live. That's why they call it "making a living." If you live simply, with fewer bills, you don't need to make as many dollars. But, income is still a need and should be kept high on the priority list.

Some of our neighbors have full-time jobs and steady paychecks with benefits, but others, like us, don't. Several commute a few miles to jobs in nearby towns. Full-time job opportunities in our rural area include the following:

- **Large-scale Farming**
- **Dairy Industries**
- **Vegetable Canning**
- **Sand Mining**
- **Light Industrial**
- **Retail/Restaurants**

Since the advent of computers, I believe we have more opportunities than ever to quit the day-job and earn a decent living from home (or car) as either a freelancer, part-time employee, or Jack (or Jill) of all trades. People who know how to fix things are currently in high demand (and will likely be so in the future). Here are some ways our inventive rural neighbors have found to earn a sustainable income as sole-proprietors of their own business enterprises:

- **Niche Farming** (sheep, fish, mushrooms, vegetables, etc)
- **Carpentry**
- **Masonry**
- **Welding**
- **Lumber Milling**
- **Trucking**
- **Excavating/Snowplowing**

Income opportunities abound these days, but who knows for how long? Here are a few more income-streams that are now being utilized by many, especially younger folks:

- **Innkeeper** (Airbnb, Hip Camp)
- **Taxi Driver** (Uber, etc)
- **On-Line Merchant** (Craigslist, Amazon, Ebay, Etsy)
- **Influencer** (Instagram, YouTube, Facebook, TikTok, etc.)

# DOMESTICATED ANIMALS

Lots of farmers near us make a living from raising animals for meat or dairy products. These include cows, chickens, pigs, sheep, even buffalo and elk. It's a hard way to earn a living as a full time farmer, but some do. Others simply have a few of each animal for meat and dairy, or just as pets. All are fine as long as the animals aren't causing more harm than good.

Back in the early 20th Century, Aldo Leopold warned against the common practice of raising cattle in your woods. They eat all of the underbrush and eventually kill the trees and drive away beneficial wildlife. Nowadays, we have better farming practices and a lot of wildlife species have returned. Nevertheless, there's still plenty of room (and need) for improvement.

## Dogs and Cats

Several friends have asked us: *"When are you going to get a dog?"* We say, *"As soon as we need one."* We have both been "pet owners" during our lives. Not sure who owned who, but I raised two dogs and Veronica raised a dog and three cats. We both loved our pets but we now love our wild animals just as much.

The introduction of even one dog or cat can change the dynamics of a wild place. If you like to photograph wildlife, a dog might chase 'em off and keep 'em away. If you like to bird-watch, even one cat left outside can put a dent in the native bird population. How many local birds do cats take out per year in the USA? I don't even want to tell you, but if you care, look it up.

It used to be that all domesticated animals including cat & dog breeds, had a specific job (other than to be cuddly). Cats controlled the mice attracted to our food reserves. Dogs controlled other larger varmints, warned us of danger and chased-away predators. Some dog breeds helped us hunt, others herded our livestock, while others saved us from drowning... *"Good dog!"*

Fast forward to today when a cat and dog's primary job is that of personal therapist. There's nothing wrong with having a loving life-force around, but they are no longer the survival need that they used to be... and they are not without cost. My dog once needed to have a tooth extraction and the vet bill was $350. In addition to pet food costs, large vet bills create a moral quandary if you're living lean. So when it comes to pets, are they wants or needs? Could be both.

# GUNS

In the days of the pioneers, (non-native) people absolutely needed guns for survival. They needed to shoot wild game for food, protect livestock and protect themselves from attack (animal and human).

Now that we've removed most of the immediate threats and food is more accessible, hunting has become more of a want/hobby than a subsistence need. Yup, there are exceptions and some do need a gun for survival. As for me, I don't hunt with a gun (a camera works) but I do own a gun. Sometimes I dust it off for target

shooting with friends. However, I have never once really needed a gun during my 60+ years on Earth. And yeah, I've had one pointed at me.

From watching old movies (like *Old Yeller*), some folks have gotten the impression that if you live in the wild, you need to be on constant watch for wild animal attacks. Wolves, bears and other *boogey-animals* might be an issue in some remote areas, but confrontations are rarer than you might think. Fuzzy predators mostly travel at night and want absolutely nothing to do with us humans. I, for one, don't blame 'em.

Ok, problems with critters might arise if you get lazy and leave meaty scraps (snacks) outside. Yes, mayhem might arise if your dog chases a bear cub up a tree. But contact is very rare because any predator is going to beat-feet outta there whenever they see, hear or smell you. There have been exceptions though…people get hit by meteorites too, but the chances are low.

*Whenever hiking in the wild, we simply walk loudly and carry a big stick.*

*…especially during early spring and the summer berry season!*

Over the past 10 years, I've had close encounters with deer, a silver fox, a fisher cat and more than one raccoon. They each briefly stared at me, then *"POOF"* they were gone. What amazing and memorable experiences! Each time, I had been walking quietly and must have caught 'em off-guard. Wild animals won't mess with you unless you mess with them! If you give them plenty of respect and room to flee, they will.

So, at the risk of being booed, I'll say it again… unless you're in constant danger of attack (and I truly hope you're not) I don't think that you need a gun. Once again, you decide.

## EVERYTHING ELSE

Once all of your needs have been met, the rest are wants. Well, whataya want? If you want everything, that'll be a problem. It's pretty easy to out-spend any amount of income.

When it comes to wants, the list can seem endless but only you know when enough's enough. If you continuously see your glass as empty or only half full, maybe choose a smaller glass. Or, drink slower?

Hobbies, vacations, restaurant dining and entertainment all have obvious benefits, but often high costs. Are these recreational items wants or needs? The answer is *"Yes."* Just don't spend all your money on fun. That's no fun.

# CHAPTER 4

# WHY GO OFF?

# PLAN B

Everyone should have a Plan B or at least give the following questions some serious thought — *"What's my next move if the sh\*t hits the fan (SHTF)? What if I lose my job, mobility, health, etc.? What'll I do?"*

Yes, what will you do? Instead of over-worrying (or over-ignoring), envision a Plan B, C and even D in case of emergency. Writing it down in detail really helps. Any plan is better than no plan. If your Plan B is to move in with your parents or kids, better develop a Plan C!

Before I get into environmental reasons for going off-grid, let me confess that my main reason was simple and somewhat selfish: I wanted to gain more financial freedom and security while living a more active and healthy lifestyle.

A large percentage of all people live paycheck-to-paycheck with heavy debt loads. Walking that financial tightrope is continually stressful.

A stiff breeze in the form of economic recession or job loss can knock you off that rope. It's happened to many hard-working people, especially during a national or worldwide recession.

The Great Recession of 2008-10 was a wake-up call for me. After witnessing four families on our block lose their homes to foreclosure, I knew we needed to establish a solid Plan B in case things got further out of our control. In 2010, we initiated our Plan B by clearing a small spot of land for a cabin and outhouse. By 2017, it was time to go! I told friends, *"I'm not a Doomsdayer, but I have a strong sense of impending Dumb."*

## Financial Freedom and Security

The easiest way to save money is simple: spend less than you earn. Ok, not so simple, especially when costs continually increase while income stagnates or declines. If you can't seem to earn more than you spend, there's only one viable option left. No, it isn't racking up more debt on credit cards and hoping to earn more in the future. That way of living is continuously stressful and simply unsustainable.

Eventually, you will have to find a way to spend less or face a life of

debt, bad credit, high-interest rates, late fees and credit hassles. Who needs that kind of non-stop stress?

*"If you find yourself in a hole, stop digging."*
— Will Rogers

We were able to lower our monthly overhead by 55% and that allowed us to pay off debts and keep more in savings. The result is that we don't have to use credit to pay for unforeseen necessities such as car repairs and dental work. If or when the SHTF, you will have more resources freed-up to meet the challenges.

After several decades of digging a ditch of debt, it is greatly freeing not having to panic every month when the "big bills" are due. The bottom line for everyone is that you gotta somehow "hoe your own row" and figure out how to make income exceed expenses…and that's no small feat. If you can accomplish this, confidence will grow and stress diminish.

*"If at first you don't succeed… then you're running about average."*
— M.H. Alderson

# HEALTH BENEFITS

It used to be that after a full day's work, a person needed rest... now, they need exercise! Did you know that some of the healthiest (and oldest) cultural groups on earth don't have a word for "exercise?" What we call exercise is just part of their everyday living. The problem with many fuel-hungry, labor-saving devices is that they eliminate the need for labor... and strenuous labor is roughly equivalent to exercise.

There's no need for a workout if you get enough exercise by working and walking. For us, health club memberships are a thing of the past. Our workout routine includes firewood preparation, water collection, garden work as well as a lot of walking.

As a mental health bonus, living within the natural world has a calming, nurturing effect that helps alleviate mental heath issues and even solves problems.

### Solitude v. Isolation

When I first watched Dick Proenneke's *Alone in the Wilderness*, I wondered if Dick got lonely. He didn't seem to mind it, but I dunno. That brings up the difference between solitude and isolation. First, I believe that the former is good, while the latter is bad. The best definition of solitude I've found is, *"temporary freedom from other people's minds."* We all need solitude to rest our monkey-minds and to help put things in perspective. Unfortunately, people get little or no solitude these days. We are constantly being bombarded with advertisements, offers, opinions, drama, bad news and spam. Too much unwanted and unneeded input! If you walk in the woods while peeking at your smartphone, that's not really solitude either. Real solitude is peaceful, restful, recuperative, regenerative… and real nice. Trivial BS just seems to melt away!

On the other hand, isolation can be destructive, demoralizing and depressing. Even if you're an introvert, you still need contact with others to remind you that you're not alone in your struggles (and triumphs).

*"We allow our ignorance to prevail upon us to make us think we can survive alone, alone in patches, alone in groups, alone in races, even alone in genders."*

— Maya Angelou

### Shinrin Yoku
(Japanese for Forest Bathing)

This is a natural therapy of walking through the forest to improve mental and physical health. It's been shown to reduce depression and increase recovery time after an injury or surgery.

Instead of the term *"Forest Bathing"* (which might wrongly imply nudity), I propose the acronym FIT (Forest Immersion Therapy). Whatever you call it, the health benefits of strolling through the forest are well documented. How it works is still being studied but it seems to work for us!

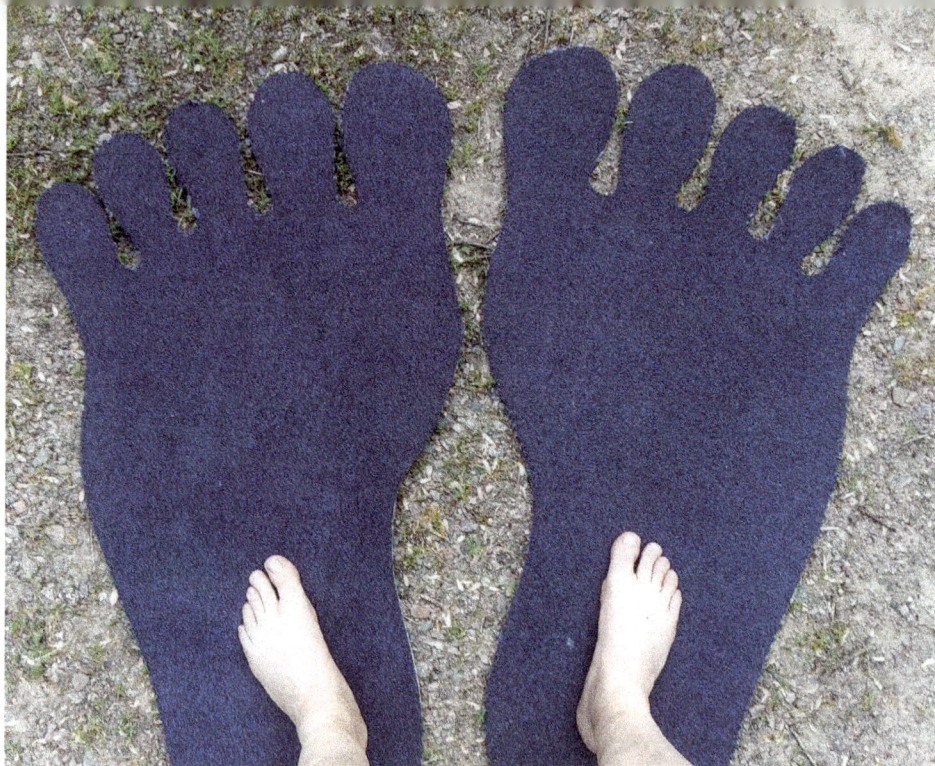

# ENVIRONMENTAL BENEFITS

Scientists and engineers continue to improve the efficiency of existing technologies and invent new technologies aimed at reducing energy consumption. For example, LED lighting has greatly reduced the cost of illumination, thus reducing electric energy use and carbon emissions.

We can hope that further advances in technology will lead to similar success stories but the sad fact is that we are still leaving a bigger and deeper "footprint" than our not-so-distant ancestors. We have more living space per person and more comfort and convenience than ever before...but this all comes at an environmental cost.

The solution to our global warming problem is far from simple and will be difficult to overcome. We can try to ignore it but it isn't going away. The issue needs to be addressed in hundreds of ways and it won't be cheap or easy. The good news is that thousands of our best and brightest scientists and citizens are working diligently on the problem from every conceivable angle.

At the very least, each of us can reduce energy use or waste by making wise choices. Combining old-school knowledge with modern technology where appropriate, we can live and work comfortably by doing more with less. By reducing energy use, we'll also save money while reducing our carbon footprints.

**Will you save the world by yourself?** Probably not. However, you will take comfort from the fact that you're fighting the good fight. If you want to get more involved, join us! There are many options. Here are some (but not all) ideas for getting more involved to help nurture nature:

- Pick up trash
- Plant a tree
- Hug a tree
- Waste less food
- Plant a garden
- Shrink your lawn
- Use less plastic
- Share a vehicle
- Ride a bus, bike or train
- Use nasty chemicals sparingly
- Promote the birds & bees

- Write your legislators
- Write to companies
- Study environmental sciences
- Work as a solar systems installer
- Be inspired
- Inspire
- Volunteer
- Vote
- Voice
- eVolve

*"We don't inherit the earth from our ancestors,*
*we borrow it from our children."*
— Native American proverb

*Nature has been for me, for as long as I remember, a source of solace, inspiration, adventure and delight; a home, a teacher, a companion.*"
— Lorraine Anderson

# CHAPTER 5

# BRAIN BASICS

Yup, in this chapter I'm going in deep! And off-grid or not, training your brain is much too important to overlook, especially when attempting a life-changing transition.

The biggest obstacles in my life have been the self-imposed mental ones. Doubts and fears have served to keep me safe, but at times they became impediments to progress and growth. I still have doubts and fears but learned to balance them with creativity and thankfulness.

Yup, I'm going in deep in this chapter but,
*"Thar's gold in them thar hills."*

# STREAMLINE & SIMPLIFY

Living within a cluttered environment can really mess with your overall feeling of peace and contentment. Too many things to look at can lead to feelings of unease. Clearing unnecessary clutter always frees my mind... and makes my day!

### Limit Your *Sh\*t*

There's a good reason why I chose the more vulgar *Sh\*t* over the milder version, *Stuff.* To me, *Stuff* has some remaining use or value. *Sh\*t* has little or no remaining value. We don't wanna look at it, smell it or step through it. Examples: cardboard boxes, plastic containers, scraps of paper and leftovers no one is ever gonna eat.

### Limit Your *Stuff* Too

By limiting possessions we are not only eliminating clutter, we're freeing up more space for living. Recently, there's been an upswing in rental storage space. Americans are moving more than ever before, so a storage space might be just the thing for transitioning from one place to another. It's a great idea if you use storage space wisely. On the other hand, paying $200/month to store $500 worth of *stuff* is not a wise use of your money.

I've read about people who have established a set limit on possessions. Some have set that number at 100. Wow, that's a commitment to a small footprint...and we are not worthy! Maybe 500 is a more achievable goal. *"Hey darling, we need another car, so let's sell the butter knife!"*

### Limit Air Space

If you removed all the air and squashed all the stuff in your room into a cube, it'd probably fit into one corner. Likewise if you put things away or pack 'em into totes and filing cabinets, they take up way less air space than piles of random debris and half-empty cardboard boxes.

### Organize Your Tools

Make sure tools used most are easily visible and accessible. Mine are in a toolbox located by the back door. Our most-used cooking tools are within reach, on or near the kitchen countertop. The rest are put away with seldom-used items tucked into the backs of the drawers, shelves, etc.

When you're deep in thought trying to build something, tools can (and do) get lost and you will waste time looking for them. If you keep all your "Essential Tools" nearby in one portable toolbox, then you'll spend less time wandering around in frustration.

# DETERMINE TO BE DETERMINED

If you've got determination, congratulations! Education is great, skills even better, but only **Determination** and its sisters, **Perseverance** and **Patience**, will ensure your success. You'll be periodically tempted to quit. But don't quit, just take a nap til that overwhelmed feeling passes, then carry on. Follow each step backward with two steps forward.

*"Never give up, for that is just the place and time that the tide will turn."*

— Harriet Beecher Stowe

Before you embark on any life-changing journey make sure you've done your research, set goals and planned your attack. That said, there is a time to overcome your own doubts and ignore the naysayers. At some point you must temporarily set aside any remaining reservations and go for it! Just tell your inner (and outer) critics to pipe down and chill.

The old saying goes, *"Follow your bliss."* Another variant is, *"Follow your bliss, but don't quit your day job."* I think that both are right, although the second is more practical. Even though the concept of off-grid life may really appeal to you, make sure you've done your homework and legwork first. If you jump in too soon, you will learn fast but you and/or your partner may not enjoy the process. The process should be part of the fun!

*"Clear your mind of can't."*

— Solon

# DON'T WASTE YOUR TIME

I think we all know that we spend too much time in front of some high-tech visual device. First it was television, now it includes computers, smartphones and anything with an LED screen. It's a wonder we get anything done!

In addition to wasting time on the phone or other devices, we can also waste weeks, months or years just spinning our wheels while focusing on the unnecessary. Here are some tips...

## Start and Finish

The two most important parts of any project are starting and finishing. It has been said: *"A job begun is a job half done."* To that I would add, *"A job not done is no good for no one."* If you're self-employed, a job not done means you don't get paid and miss the rent payment. When it comes to building your own shelter, a job not done means you get wet and/or freeze your butt!

## Perfect v. Good Enough

If you're primarily a perfectionist (like me), there's always a mental struggle between finishing and making it perfect. I tend to agree with the quote:

*"Perfect is the enemy of good."*

— Voltaire

Balance between quality and time is the goal. As an artist and engineer, I know that art is mostly about form while engineering is about balancing pros and cons. The function of art is to please the artist and others through aesthetic arrest. An engineer not only has to make it right, he or she must make it **just** right. They can design a car that lasts a million miles, but it'll cost you a million dollars (or so). Don't get me wrong, you should always strive for excellence when working for others. But if it's just for you, a labor- of-love, then it's ok to cut some aesthetic corners, especially if it reduces costs and impacts.

*"Have the courage to be imperfect!"*

— Alfred Adler

## Second Opinions

Some DIYers like to do it ALL themselves. That's cool, but can involve extra trial and error. We stubbornly struggle (and complain) rather than ask others for insights toward a better way. Why invent the wheel when someone's already done so? Why waste time and effort when an easier, cheaper, better way might be within reach? The perfect idea or solution may be hiding in the brain of a trusted friend, waiting to be discovered. Just ask!

## Avoid the "Con"

Sadly, there are some folks out there who have no qualms about lying, cheating or stealing to satisfy their wants and needs...always has been, probably always will be. Some never buy into that whole

Golden Rule thing. **First:** Don't be one of them. **Second:** Try not to fall for their Con. Common sense and critical thinking go a very long way.

> *"It is easier to fool someone, than to convince them they've been fooled."*
> — Mark Twain

Be friendly yet skeptical when entering into any agreement, whether verbal or written. Do your research, ask around and give folks the benefit of doubt. If you are later tricked or conned, don't spend all of your time ruminating about it. Do what you can, learn your lesson, then move on to more constructive things.

I've been conned and robbed a couple of times. I admit it. All water under the bridge now! My advice is to avoid Narcissists, Negative Nellies and Nonsense… and whatever you do, don't follow any Pied Piper into the water.

## Think Like a (Good) Juror

Realize that every human brain contains numerous biases and we should fight their influences. Confirmation Bias is particularly inherent, infectious and rampant, especially in the political realm. It can and should be kept in check when making important decisions. Very few issues are black and white (or red and blue). I freely admit that I've carried some strong convictions for decades only to discover that my thinking had been flawed and counterproductive. Without good sense and critical thinking, we often make things worse for ourselves and others. Magical thinking is ok, but only if it doesn't create more problems. Personally, **I'd rather invoke my right to ignorance** than to take a hard stance on anything. Only when I've researched all arguments will I take a medium stance, especially on complicated and controversial topics. No need to argue vociferously, My job as a juror is to learn and decide.

> *"To be wronged s nothing unless you continue to remember it."*
> — Confucius

Photo by Linda Eichacher

## MATTER V. DON'T MATTER

Remember Steve Jobs' words of wisdom: *"Don't let something that doesn't matter cause you to lose something that does."* So, what really matters? Well, the needs we covered in chapters 2 & 3 definitely matter, but so do love, health and other things.

Here's a short list of those **things that matter** to most healthy human beings:

- ○ Intimacy
- ○ Friendships
- ○ Meaningful material objects
- ○ Money
- ○ Health
- ○ Rewarding work
- ○ Security
- ○ Freedom
- ○ Affirmation
- ○ Rejuvenating recreation

There are other **things that matter to some but not all to the same extent.**

- ○ Creativity
- ○ Spirituality

**What doesn't matter?**

- ○ Things you have no way to control
- ○ Petty grievances
- ○ Foolish pride

## ROLLING WITH PUNCHES

You don't have to be Nostradamus to predict, with confidence, that there will be hard times in the future (aka punches)… both light punches and hard ones. If you've already been hit hard and survived, then you know that you're resilient. *"Humans are a resilient breed but one never knows how resilient until one is tested."* Perhaps, that is why older folks are generally happier and more content than younger adults. The elders have been punched plenty and have persevered. My message here is that there is hope for a better future. Look for solutions, get busy… and roll!

Ever have one of those days, weeks, months or years? Times when you were just plain unhappy and discontented, even depressed? I have. Like many of you, I've struggled with anxiety and depression for more years than I'd like to admit. I'm not struggling nearly as much as before. One big reason is that I've learned some simple tricks to *"De-Funk"* myself as needed. At first glance they seem too simple, but check 'em out below. If you find yourself stuck in *"Funky Town,"* there are ways to get yourself out.

*"Better to light a candle than to curse the darkness."*

— Chinese Proverb

**Did ya Know?** Historians rate 2020 as only the 8th worst year in American History and only the 6th worst in World History. You can debate the numbers but the point is that we've all survived bigger punches. Consider the Civil War, two World Wars and The Great Depression. During my lifetime, 1962-4, 1968 and 2001-2 were pretty tumultuous years too. 2008 was no picnic either.... yet here we are.

# RELEASING NEGATIVE EMOTIONS

Almost 20 years ago, I read a book entitled "The Sedona Method." It's built on the premise that emotions are not part of you or your mind, but rather temporary and detachable feelings. They are simply our brain's biochemical responses to stress. These chemicals can get out of control and ruin your entire day (not to mention the day of people around you).

Here are a few negative emotions ranging from bad to worse: worry, shame, guilt, jealousy, fear, anger and rage.

Yeah, these feelings are unpleasant but are all designed by God or Nature to help us survive. The problem is that an overload of negative thoughts can instantly change your mood, even if there's really nothing wrong. The good news is that negative thoughts and emotions are not attached to us. They can be noticed and dislodged (like gum on your shoe) by using the following visual-imaging method that I adapted from the Sedona method.

*People become attached to their burdens sometimes more than the burdens are attached to them."*
–George Bernard Shaw

Photo-collaboration with Sean Doyle

### Release your negative emotions:

1. Grab some paper and write down how you feel on a scale of 0-10.
2. Write down what's really bugging you.
3. Crumple the paper and hold it tightly in one hand.
4. Imagine that your negative emotion (feeling) is now contained in that wad of paper.
5. Keep squeezing til uncomfortable, then slowly release your grip and let the paper fall.

Nobody else needs to see what you've written and you can let it fall into the wastebasket, or better yet, use it as a fire-starter. Sometimes, you have to go through the process more than once because well-entrenched ruminations can be stubborn. Don't fret, just try it again. Many folks like me say it works! Might seem like hocus-pocus, but it's really an effective visual-mental exercise to calm your mind.

This method is no replacement for professional mental health care but it's a good way to do some effective mental health self-help. Even if you don't always go through the above steps, just the knowledge that your emotions are detachable can help to ease your mind. Simply be aware that you are not your emotions. Emotions are like clouds of consciousness moving through us… just let them move through and float away. *"Buh Bye."*

## Talking Back To Negative Self-Talk

According to psychological research, the average human has literally thousands of thoughts per day, most of which are negative. A negative thought is any thought that makes you cringe, frown or sigh (a little or a lot). The latest estimate is 4,000-5,000 negative thoughts per person per day. Yes, hard to believe…

No wonder we're depressed!

Negative thoughts typically last from a one to several seconds at a time and can really add up on a stressful day. Any thoughts dealing with past failures, current difficulties or future doom can be considered negative. They often involve four-letter words and words like can't, should and wish. Three clear examples of negative thoughts are: *I wish my life didn't suck — I'll never be able to do this — and — #&$@%!*

Negative self-talk is also referred to as our *"Inner Critic."* Other names can also be used. *"Debbie or Donny Downer"* comes to mind. You can silence this nagging voice by simply talking back to it.

For example, when you ask, *"Why me?,"* you respond to yourself, *"Why not me?"* When you think *"I'm just a loser"* you respond, *"I disagree. You're having a rough week. You've been through worse and overcame it!"* You can think of this more positive and reassuring voice as your *"Inner Defense Attorney"* or *"Voice of Reason"*.

No matter how we process the outside world, each of us has both positive and negative inner thoughts, and each side is engaged in an epic courtroom battle to sway the jury. The bottom line is to realize that we each have the ability to minimize our negative thoughts. All it takes is balance, mindfulness and practice. I think it's easier done than said!

# BASICS OF CONTENTMENT

This section applies whether you live off grid or not. In fact, it doesn't matter who you are, what you look like, who you love or where you've been... we could all use a little more contentment! This is something that not even lottery winners or CEOs easily attain and I believe it's a very important concept for any lifestyle, rural or urban.

*"Wealth consists not in having great possessions but in having few wants."*

— Esther de Waal

There's been a lot written about success and happiness. Just take a peek in the self-help section of any book store. I've read some of those books and now believe that success and happiness have been somewhat overrated, with contentment being a more attainable goal. What is success? Can you be happy all of the time? Are you happy while doing your taxes, or during dental work?

For one thing, we're still living with an antiquated model of success. It involves primarily money, power, fame and toys. We've spent too much time keeping up with the Joneses, and they are usually no more content than we are. It is possible to become financially successful but utterly fail in other meaningful ways.

Whoever dies with the most toys wins? I beg to differ. I believe that making your way toward overall contentment (without abusing others) should be a key component of the new definition of success. It might sound radical, but the concept has been around for Millenia. Personally, I'd rather be a content carpenter than a miserable millionaire.

What I mean to say, is that we've all spun out of control and continue to do so from time to time. I'm here to say that each of us has the ability to make things better. Every now and then, we can and should do some maintenance on our soul. When feeling out of sorts for more than a few days, I recommend taking the following contentment quiz. I borrowed the concept from a book I read 20+ years ago and have since used it to find out which important areas could use improvement. It's helps me know what's really bugging me so I can work on ways toward better emotional balance.

If all your scores are high, then you're probably relatively content. If some or all of your scores are low, don't despair, it simply shows the key areas where you need improvement. Just knowing helps. From there, you can adjust priorities and make some plans to raise those numbers. Even if you don't take immediate action to improve low scores, your subconscious mind will work behind the scenes to come up with solutions for more contentment.

## TAKE THE QUIZ

Simply rate each one of the following aspects of your life. How happy are you with each one?

**Miserable** gets a 0 and **Fully Content** gets a 10... **So-So** gets a 5.

Your scaling system may be different from others but it doesn't matter. Just score each honestly and you'll quickly see where you could use improvement.

**Q:** Does anyone ever spiral into control?

**A:** Yes, but it takes longer.

| Contentment Quiz | |
|---|---|
| **Things That Matter** (Core Values) | **Today's Score** (0 to 10 scale) |
| Intimacy (I) | |
| Friendships (F) | |
| Meaningful Material Objects (MMO) | |
| Money ($) | |
| Health (H) | |
| Rewarding Work (RW) | |
| Security (S) | |
| Freedom (F) | |
| Affirmation (A) | |
| Renewing Recreation (RR) | |
| Spirituality (S) | |
| Creativity (C) | |

A better way to visualize this quiz is to plot each aspect as a spoke on a wheel. Together the spokes make a wheel that represents your emotional life. A large round wheel is more stable than a small uneven one. This visual device helps you see which aspect of your life (what's important to you) needs improvement and where it doesn't. Hills are ok but valleys reveal areas which could use attention. The goal is to build a nice big round wagon wheel shape so your life rotates smoothly.

**SCORING 0-10**
Center Dot = 0
Outer Ring = 10

**Example A:**
Good

**Example B:**
Not so good

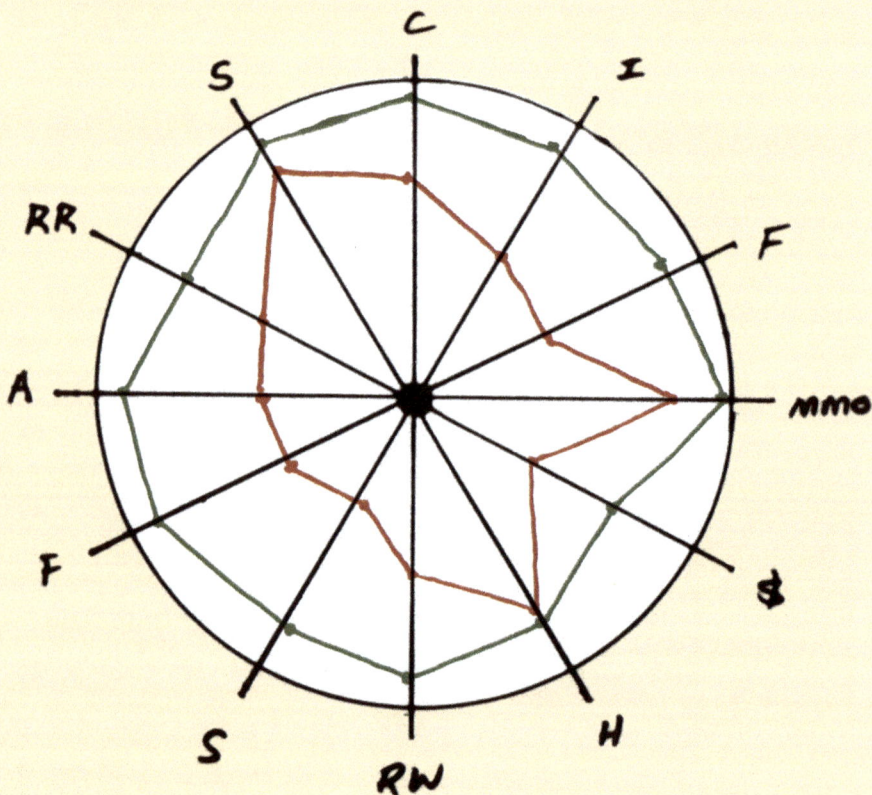

Examples A and B were me on two different days, a few years apart.

To summarize everything in this chapter, I will leave you with three of my personal favorite sayings, the last of which is on T-shirts and bumper stickers everywhere.

*Learn from the past, Live the present, Create the future.*

*"Be yourself. Everyone else is taken."* – Oscar Wilde

*Life is Short. Don't be a Dick.\** — Unknown
*\*Be more like Dick Proenneke*

# CHAPTER 6

# MORE OFF GRID TIPS

# RESEARCH EVERYTHING

For basic research, you can ask friends, seek experts, read books or check magazines. A faster way to do research is online. You can become an instant expert (or at least well-informed) on just about any topic. Granted, you won't become a brain surgeon, but you certainly can learn key concepts and details. There's hardly a question I haven't been able to answer after an hour or so of online investigation *(surfing)*.

People ask me if I'm a carpenter or if I knew how to build a house before I started. I tell them *"absolutely not, but I found out!"* After viewing YouTube tutorials and asking freelance carpenters, I was ready for action. Later, I simply learned by doing. Occasionally, I'd check online tutorials when I got stuck or frustrated. From there it was non-stop action for several months. My Mantra: *Plan, Do, Rinse, Repeat!* You don't have to be an expert but you will become one by the time you've finished!

### Become a Search Engineer

For years, Google has been the place to search for anything but some don't like the way it keeps track of your activities.

Another option is Duck Duck Go, which doesn't track your information. Learn how to use keywords and narrow your searches by year, state, etc.

### YouTube It

YouTube has been around for less than two decades but it has already revolutionized online learning. You can find anything from auto repair to rocket science on YouTube.

### Wikipedia for Primer

If you don't know anything about a subject, the first place to start is Wikipedia. It's a great platform to get all sides of the story, even the controversial parts. After all, *"Truth Geeks"* are controlling it.

### Keep an Eye on FRED

I think it's a good idea to periodically visit the Federal Reserve Education Division (FRED) website to view the current trajectory of the US economy. It's a good way to check which way the wind's-a-blowin'. As self-employed individuals, Veronica and I have felt the economic pressure of the past 3 recessions. We've

**If you're planning on a big purchase or big sale, it's a good idea to check with good ole FRED!** https://fred.stlouisfed.org/series/UNRATE

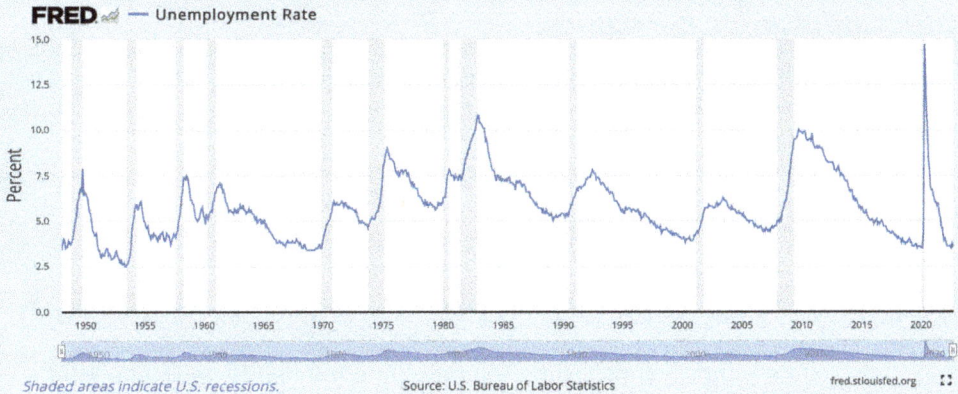

Shaded areas indicate U.S. recessions.    Source: U.S. Bureau of Labor Statistics    fred.stlouisfed.org

learned that (paying) work periodically slows down and even dries up…Uh-oh!

Recessions are bad for some but can open opportunities for others. In general, it is usually the best time to buy stuff like cars and real estate. Folks with accumulated wealth (and gamblers with credit) tend to buy-buy-buy during a recession, while the rest of us sell anything worth value (often for pennies on the dollar). It's a real bummer when a work slowdown happens to you but you can prepare yourself for the next recession by reviewing where we've been as a Country. (See chart above.)

# BECOME A SCROUNGE-MASTER

Merriam Webster states the definition of *"scrounge"* as *"to get as needed by or as if by foraging, scavenging, or borrowing."* When

striving to live simply and frugally, just become good at scrounging and you'll save a fortune.

Realize that a lot of raw materials, water and fuel go into the manufacturing of every tool, toy or trinket. Most, if not all, of their impacts have already occurred. That's why we always search for used items and materials first. Wise DIY'ers seek for novel ways to use and repair what they already own, then seek used items if available. Why buy new when used will do?

Nowadays, everyone knows what *"Dumpster Diving"* is. Well, becoming a "Scrounge-Master" involves diving not just dumpsters but anywhere free, useful items have been discarded. Stealing is a no-no so bring your moral compass when diving. Once I found a bucket full of lightly used hand tools worth $200 just sitting inside of an apartment complex dumpster… Yoink!

## Free Building Materials

1. **Ask around first.** Some people have lumber in their garages they'd just as soon get rid of.

2. **Check online, there's a number of sources.** (Craigslist, Free Market, FB Marketplace, Nextdoor)

3. **Check with local shipping companies.** We were able to obtain 200 lightly used 2x6s from a company that shipped PVC pipe. For free!

4. **Offer to dismantle a shed or garage in return for building materials.**

## Cheap Building Materials

**Cull Piles:** If you're preparing to build a shelter, rather than buying new lumber, it's a good idea to visit your lumber yard's cull pile where they knock the price down by seventy-five percent or more. It's lumber that's cracked, warped or simply returned.

Some lumber yards spray paint these boards to show that it's discounted.

It takes time and several visits, but occasionally you can leave the store with a thousand dollars worth of lumber for $200. It's not always obvious where it is so you might have to ask.

**Re-Use Centers:** Shop re-use centers if any are nearby. Most major cities now have them and you can find building materials, windows, and tools at a fraction of the original cost.

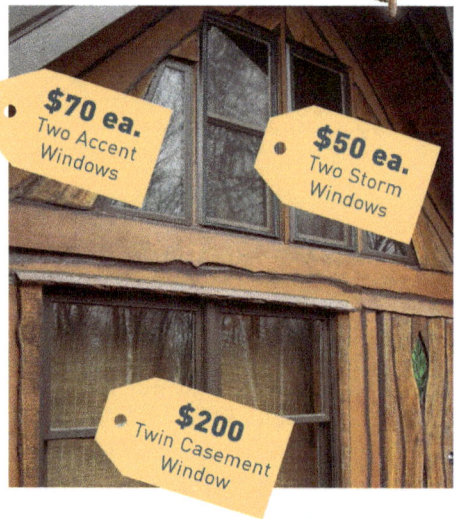

$70 ea.
Two Accent Windows

$50 ea.
Two Storm Windows

$200
Twin Casement Window

FREE
cut from our woods

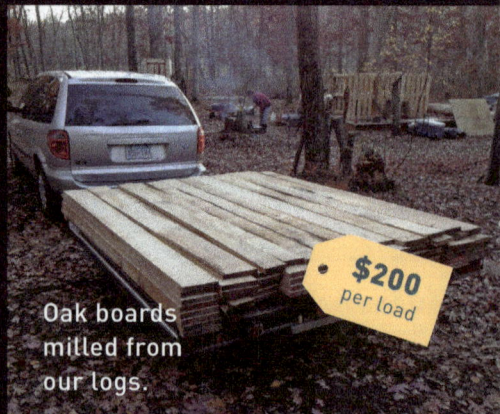

Oak boards milled from our logs.

$200
per load

**Auction sites:** Government auction sites like the General Services Administration (GSA) Auctions, as well as private auctions are other good resources.

### Online - Used Stuff
### (Craigslist/Marketplace/Ebay)

We hit these sites first to score great values at fractions of the cost of similar new items. We use them at different times, not only for shopping but often just to find out the current value of things.

### Online - New Stuff
### (Amazon or Other)

Love it, hate it, or both, Amazon is still top dog when it comes to online shopping sites. Some prefer to leap over Amazon and shop at the websites of manufacturers, vendors or retail stores. In general, Amazon has more sales, statistics and reviews so searching for best values is made easy.

A good rule of thumb for finding the best value is to first review items that have a lot of sales and a high rating. If an item has been sold 500+ times with a rating of 4.5, you have some reassurance that it'll perform above-average. Even if the written reviews are mostly good, read the bad ones too. Also, consider a used or refurbished version of that product, if the price is right.

Once you've found an item you like, you can use *"Camel Camel Camel"* to check how much its price has fluctuated over the past year. It will let you know if you should buy now or wait a few months. Simply copy the title of the product from Amazon, then paste it into the search window at camelcamelcamel.com. It provides a graph of the item's past price over time. Seasonal items such as lawn furniture or camping gear can vary widely throughout the year. Timing is everything when it comes to deals.

• $FREE

## Cabin Material Costs: $6,580

| | |
|---|---|
| Gravel | $400 |
| Lumber | $2200 |
| 14 Windows | $950 |
| 2 Doors | $0 |
| Metal Roofing | $580 |
| Foil-Faced Foam Panels | $450 |
| Tar Paper & House Wrap | $300 |
| Caulk & Foam Sealant | $450 |
| Screws, Nails & Hardware | $250 |
| Paint & Varnish | $300 |
| Wood Stove & Stove Pipe | $700 |

# SEARCHING FOR LAND

## Where to Search

The following states have the least expensive land, but you'll notice that they're not necessarily ground-water rich areas: Montana, Wyoming, Nevada, New Mexico, South Dakota, North Dakota, Idaho and Nebraska.

Prices in these States currently start at $2000 an acre but you might not be able to obtain just one at a time. Land prices in other states like Minnesota and Wisconsin start at $2500 for non-agricultural forest land. There's often a minimum land parcel size that can be bought or sold, so be sure to check local zoning regulations in the counties or townships that you're considering. **See Appendix B for more detail on buying rural land in Wisconsin.**

## Look at Lots (of Lots)

Before you have any money or plans, just start looking in those areas that are most desirable to you. Use online real estate sites as well as local papers. Sometimes nothing beats a drive through the countryside.

How many land lots should you look at? I say "lots." If you review 100 lots, you'll have a very good idea what a good deal looks like. A once-in-a-lifetime deal comes around every day... you just gotta know how to spot it, then act with haste!

## Look from Space

Once you've found some promising lots, use Google Earth to view the property's layout and surrounding land parcels. In some cases, you can even view old aerial photographs of the property from years ago.

## Look at GIS
### (Geographic Information System)

Most counties in the US provide interactive online GIS maps to the public. Not all of the GIS functionality is available in all counties without signing in, but you can find basic info like: PID (property identification) number, acreage, property lines, topography and who (or what company) owns the neighboring properties. Just type the county name and "GIS" into any search engine to locate the county's GIS site. It's not always user-friendly, but you can learn some important details with this tool.

*"Land: They're not making any more of it."*
— Ray Welder

Photo: Bruce Christianson

## Look Above and Below Ground

You can only learn so much from pictures and maps. You simply must walk the property and ask questions before you get too excited about a candidate. Many remote properties are listed for sale in no other way than a sign on the road.

If there's no clean and accessible groundwater at the site, you'll need to factor-in the additional cost of purchasing drinking water and collecting rain water.

## Look for Clean Title

Search for the titles of any property before putting money down. For extra reassurance, a surveyor can be hired to locate the legal property boundaries. Land surveys tend to be expensive but old fences or old sketches are not to be trusted. Some rural properties are tied up in covenants, which are rules that protect the land from being developed in specific ways. Un-zoned land and land zoned for agriculture usually have fewer restrictions.

## Balance Price with Everything Else

It's unlikely that any single property will check-off everything on your wish list, so this is a good time to differentiate between wants and real needs. Consider water access, cell phone coverage, distance to grocery store and other factors. Then weigh these against the price… and the awesome view!

## Pay in Cash

It should come as no surprise that many banks don't like to make loans for remote land, especially if there's not a house already on it. You may be able to get a loan for land but it will likely involve a bigger down-payment and higher rates. If you have a high credit limit you might be able to borrow enough to purchase a five acre parcel. It's expensive but so is a new car… and that car won't be worth much in 20 years!

### Questions best asked
(and answered) **before you buy:**

1. What is the history of the property?
2. Are there any property restrictions or ownership issues with minerals and timber?
3. Is the land accessible year-round, without crossing another property?
4. What are the (human, animal or corporate) neighbors like?
5. How deep (and good) is the groundwater?
6. Is the soil rocky, sandy, muddy or just right?

# MEET YOUR WILD NEIGHBORS

Now let's talk about the birds and bees... even if it seems uncomfortable.

By now everyone's heard about declining bee populations... Hey, that's not good. Who's gonna pollinate our food sources? Not everyone knows it, but native bird species are also on the decline, and it ain't because of windmills. Who cares? We all really should. Birds are not only fun to watch, they keep the bugs at bay and don't ask for much other than a safe place to raise their young.

When I was in my 20's and 30's, I didn't give much thought to wildlife. Birds, bugs, bees and furry mammals always seemed to just be "there" doing their own thing. I knew the basics: robin, cardinal, bluebird, chipmunk, squirrel etc., but didn't know much else. Nowadays, the more I learn, the more I wanna learn. These native creatures have been evolving for millennia without our help (or hindrance) and we need to promote them.

When you get to know the names and specializations of each species of plant and animal, you appreciate them more and understand how they fit into the ecosystem. You'll find yourself noticing plants you've never noticed before. One of Veronica's nieces greets each new discovery with a soft query... "Hello there. Who are you?" Now we do the same.

**Here are a few ways to meet and know your wild neighbors** (the ones not holding a beer):

- Sit quietly outside, especially at dawn and dusk
- Use color reference books
- Browse online wildlife guides (eg. Cornell.edu)
- Use wild smartphone apps
- Take wild classes

## Aldo Leopold's Golden Rule of Ecology

This famous rule still rings true 80 years after it was first printed:

*"A thing is right when it tends to preserve the integrity, stability, and beauty of the biotic community. It is wrong when it tends otherwise."*

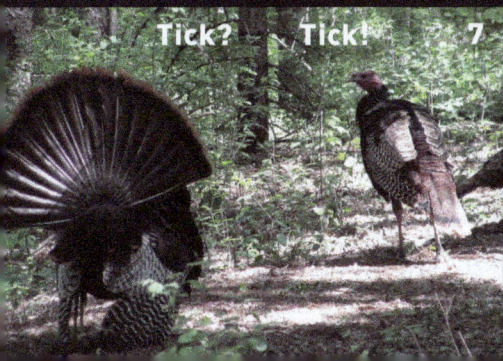

## Say Hello to Our Little Friends...

Here are a few of our favorite wild neighbors, whom we've had the pleasure to meet over the past few years. They all happily help keep the insect and rodent populations in-check and in turn, we simply leave 'em alone. We're not sure what they think of us, but we consider them good friends and neighbors!

### Aves (Birds)

1. A nocturnal mouse-population manager, the stealthy **Barred Owl** often asks, "Who Cooks For You?"

2. The flashy **Eastern Towhee** is a forest floor forager and accomplished dancer, who reminds us to, "Drink Your Tea!"

3. The large dinosaur-descended ant-eater, **Pileated Woodpecker** (Phil or Phillis around here), has a loud laughing call that inspired Woody Woodpecker.

4. **Osprey** love to fish! Once endangered like Bald Eagles and Trumpeter Swans, this species is still rare but on the comeback.

5. A head-first downhill runner, the **White-Breasted Nuthatch** is a year-round friend, named for its talent of wedging nuts into tree crevices and then pecking (hatching) 'em open.

6. Preferring to nest under rain-sheltered man-made structures, **Eastern Phoebes** are lovers not fighters. Rather than dive bomb to defend the nest they sally about with a short & cute call (Fee-Bee). These welcome guests happily feast on mosquitoes and other pesky pests in return for food and shelter.

7. Like ruffed grouse and other ground-foraging birds, **Wild Turkeys** can each eat 100's of ticks per day! We say, "Yay!"

8. The proud symbol of our country and once almost eradicated by the super-foolish use of DDT insecticides, the **Bald Eagles** are back and they're looking for food (dead or alive). They're one of the big reasons we don't see or smell as many dead fish along our shorelines.

### Amphibia (Amphibians)

9. Wisconsin's **Pickerel Frog** population is of special concern due to its specific needs and loss of habitat. Secretes a poisonous substance so No -Touchy!

10. The stealthy, fast (and handsomely masked) **Wood Frog** quacks like a duck, but isn't.

11. Mostly nocturnal, **Gray Tree Frogs** like to play peek-a-boo and can change color from grey to green for best camouflage.

12. These dark-dwelling cuties eat bugs, worms and snails making the **Red-backed Salamander** an important species of forest ecosystems.

### Mammalia (Mammals)

13. The **Fisher** (often called Fisher Cat) is not a cat but part of the weasel family. Essentially hunted and trapped out of the lower 48, its numbers are slowing improving in the northern-most states. Happy to eat almost anything including rotted meat. I call the fisher, along with coyote, raccoon, eagle and vulture, the Clean-up Crew. Thanks!

14. The common forest-dwelling **Eastern Chipmunk** can be a pesky ally. A scurry of chipmunks are sometimes loud (Chip!) and will sample a little from your garden, but they're always entertaining and effectively keep mice (and other invaders) away!

# The Pollinators

## Lepidoptera
### (Butterflies & Moths)

1. The yellow-striped **Nessus Sphinx Moth** masquerades as a big nasty wasp or hummingbird to get a long unfettered sip of sweet nectar.

2. What the...! Ok, it's the freaky pre-metamorphic version of a Tiger Swallowtail (picture 3). The **Eastern Tiger Swallowtail Caterpillar** has developed faux eyespots on the thorax as a deceptive defense.

3. The **Eastern Tiger Swallowtail Butterfly** is a well-established native inhabitant of the eastern half of North America. With long legs and proboscis (feeding tube) they can reach deep into flowers for a good glob of nectar. These features, together with large wings, make it a very efficient pollinator.

### Apis (Bees)

4. A determined **Carpenter Bee** goes to work on a Nasturtium flower. There are 13 types and 250 species of bees in our State.

5. The humble **Bumble Bee** is mellow 'til messed with.

### Give Bees a Chance

**Did ya know** that bees evolved from wasps to eat only nectar and pollen? Wasps are more aggressive hunter/scavengers that eat other insects or meat. Yellow Jackets, Baldfaced Hornets, Ground Hornets (aka Digger Wasps) and Paper Wasps are types of wasp around here. These live in colonies and the females will not hesitate to sting if the hive is threatened. Keep your distance if possible — a group of angry gals is a formidable force!

Bees, wasps and hornets are all vital components of our ecosystem. Most of us know something about Honey Bees, Bumble Bees and Sweat Bees but there are 10 additional types of bees here in the Midwest, including the docile Mason Bees which are 120 times more effective at pollination than the Bumbles. That's why farmers love 'em! Each of the 13 types contain multiple species bringing the number to roughly 250 species of bees!

Some bee species like the Digger, Masked and Cuckoo Bee, look very similar to hornets and other wasps, so before resorting to chemical warfare (insecticide, wasp spray) make sure you're giving bees a chance. Without 'em, we'd bee screwed!

# NURTURE THE NATIVES

Native plants and animals have been developing their specialties and defenses for millennia. Just to be safe, I'd say go easy on the exotic non-native flowers. The bees and insects around here are not accustomed to the nectar of a non-native ornamental plant. That's like giving an energy drink to a toddler!

Native plants are much better, more like mother's milk to bees and they come up every spring. Bee Balm, Butterfly Weed, Milkweed, Echinacea, Black-eyed Susan, etc. It has been said that *"Ignorance is bliss."* I agree… *'til it ain't!* Throughout my career as an environmental engineer, I've seen people do things to their land that ended up biting them in the butt. Disposing of used oil, collecting disease-infected firewood from other areas and not maintaining septic systems can all ruin the environment… and your day… or year.

In addition, any time you disrupt the soil you increase the likelihood of attracting unwanted invasive flora & fauna. It's quite easy to invite buckthorn, poison ivy, garlic mustard or wild parsnip just by disturbing the soil and leaving it unplanted for months. Friendly, native plants such as lambsquarter and milkweed might grow first, but a flock of buckthorn-berry-eating birds might also do a fly-by!

# PESKY PESTS

Ok, this might seem like a deal-breaker for some, but Pesky Pests are everywhere, both in cities and in the wild. You can freak out if you need to, but there are options. You can avoid and/or live with the peskiest of pests. If you learn when they're most active and how to deal with them, then they're no biggie, just another seasonal inconvenience.

You can just stay in a screened porch all summer but you'll have to venture into the hungry insect world eventually. Some bug repellents work and some don't. Everyone has a different attractiveness-factor based on individual size, skin temperature, odor, etc. Here are a few things that we and/or our friends have tried.

### DYI Bug Repellants
Essential oils in spray bottles work well but need to be applied often. Try Lavender, Camphor, Cloves, Cinnamon, Catnip, Marigolds, Eucalyptus, Peppermint, Lemongrass or Citronella.

### Commercial Bug Repellants
3M Ultrathon and Deep Woods Off both contain DEET and work quite well. We have not tested the effectiveness of each brand of repellants but others have. Each person attracts biting bugs differently, so do your own research. To insects, I'm considered prime beef!

### DIY Mouse Repellants
Moth Balls, Peppermint, Cayenne Pepper are effective deterrents. Also, make sure all doors are well-sealed at the bottom. This is the most common entry point for mice. If you can see daylight under the door, that's not much of a squeeze for them.

| Pest | When Most Active | How to Deal |
|------|------------------|-------------|
| **Mice** | Autumn | Mothballs or peppermint oil under doors |
| **Mosquitoes** | Summer after rains | Screens, repellants, treated clothing* |
| **No-See-Ums** | Spring and summer | Screens, repellants, treated clothing* |
| **Flies** | Mid to late summer | Screens, swatters, no food or bevies outside! |
| **Ticks** | Spring (They like it cool, not hot.) | Repellants, white or treated clothing*, "Tick Checks" (see next page). |
| **Spiders** | Summer | Take 'em outside or leave 'em be. They eat other bugs. |
| **Hornets/Wasps** | Late summer/autumn | Leave 'em alone if possible. |

* Clothing treated with Permethrin.

Our choice for trapping indoor mice (Sorry Dudes!) is the mostly plastic *"Better Mousetrap"* design. It's relatively humane and easy to set & release. We think it's more effective (and less gross) than old-fashioned spring traps. If you don't want to catch toads and chipmunks (and trust me, you don't) use this trap inside and away from doors. Poisons and sticky traps should also be avoided. These methods work but are ultimately… more unpleasant.

## Nature's Insect Control

Once again, if we didn't have birds, frogs and bats, we'd all be overrun with insects, especially mosquitoes and flies. The mosquitoes around our former suburban home were out of control in summer. You could hardly walk from house to car without getting a bite or two. We actually suffer fewer of these bugs now that we live in an area abundant with bug-eaters.

**I used to consider most crawling or flying insects to be pesky pests. Now I know better.** If you're afraid of creepy-crawlies, turn your fear into curiosity! Instead of freaking out at the sight of a bug, take a photo and get to know your tiny neighbor. Here's a short list of fascinating insects that we have observed & researched while living off-grid. If you like having your mind blown, check out these precious little buggers!

- Springtails
- Fireflies
- Mason Bees
- Wolf Spiders
- Walking Sticks
- Sargent Beetles

## Tick Checks

Check yourself for ticks every evening before bed and again in the morning. A mirror and/or your partner is quite helpful in this endeavor.

**Blacklegged Tick (Deer Tick)**

Female Adult    Male Adult    Nymph   Larva

## Deer Ticks (blacklegged ticks or ixodes scapularis)

are tiny parasites that sometimes carry Lyme's disease and other bacterial infections. However, they have to be attached for 24-48 hours to pass Lyme's to us. Therefore, we make it a habit to check thoroughly during the worst weeks, usually late April through early June. It's no fun to pick an attached tick off yourself, your friend or your pet, but they sell handy-dandy "Tick Picks" that make this task a bit easier.

Once the tick is out, just wet the area with hydrogen peroxide. If a red ring develops it doesn't necessarily mean you have Lyme's Disease. If the ring persists and grows, it's a good idea to check with a doctor or nurse. It could be a bacterial infection other than Lyme's, but still may require an antibiotic treatment. Around here, the deer population is at record levels and so is the deer tick population. That is why we take tick checks seriously. Inconvenient? Somewhat. Worthy of panic? Not really.

SOURCE: *Materials developed by the CDC. The tick photo and illustration from the website CDC.gov does not imply endorsement by the CDC or the United States Government of this publication Forth To Basics.*

# BEING NEIGHBORLY

As the name *"do-it-yourselfer"* implies, DIYers like to do it themselves. That's cool but sometimes you can't do it all by yourself, especially in remote areas and during emergencies. You'll be glad if you have friends and allies nearby, so it's a very good idea to meet your neighbors before you start any kind of construction (or loud activity). Yeah, they may look or act *"different."* Just suck it up and make the effort. Either write, call, text, or better yet, meet them in person if you see them working outside.

Some would rather not drive up to a secluded house and knock on the door. I don't blame you. As an alternative, I recommend good old snail mail. A hand-written letter or note still carries a personal touch that can't be beat. Your first contact should never include your concerns or complaints.

Maybe your neighbors don't want to be bothered. Ok, that happens, but your efforts will not be in vain. You'll be glad you tried. Even if you don't become close friends, you can at least be friendly. It's called being *"Neighborly."*

*"Be kind, for everyone you meet is fighting a hard battle."*
— Unknown, previously attributed to Plato

The absolute worst idea is to get into conflict with your neighbors. Squabbles over fence lines, fallen trees, garbage, barking dogs, etc. are common but I recommend a more tactful *"ask-and-offer"* approach. Always be careful what you bitch for!

You never know what your neighbors have been through, or are currently going through. When in doubt, just be nice! There's simply no good reason to kick sand in someone else's stewpot!

Hey, why not expand your neighborhood? It's always a good idea to seek out new friends and neighbors (even internationally) while nurturing existing relationships. With today's modern communications it's easy to find others that have similar pursuits and interests. They may have already found *"riches in niches"* and have stories and insights to share. Use your search engine to find 'em or just visit your local Farmers Market and other events.

If you have any questions, comments or suggestions for future revisions, please kindly leave a message at **forthtobasics.com**. (You won't go on any mailing list but ours.)

## Just can't find the words?
### How 'bout these?

Hygge (hoo-gah) — Danish for enjoying the good things in life with good people — a mood of coziness and togetherness, with feelings of wellness and contentment.

Friluftsliv (free-loofts-liv) — Norwegian for *Free Air Life*, is about enjoying the uplifting ambiance of the outdoors, no matter the weather.

Hygge focuses on getting cozy with friends while Frilutsliv relates to our pleasurable dynamic with nature.

Photo: Bruce Christianson

# REFERENCES AND RECOMMENDED READING

## References

*A Sand County Almanac*
Aldo Leopold

*Norwegian Wood*
Lars Mytting

*Braiding Sweetgrass, Gathering Moss*
Robin Wall Kimmerer

*Back to Basics: A Complete Guide to Traditional Skills*
Edited by Abigail R. Gehring

*Don't Believe Everything You Think*
Thomas Kida

*7 Habits of Highly Effective People*
Stephen Covey

*The Sedona Method*
Hale Dwoskin

*The Happiness Equation*
Neil Pasricha

*Wildwood Wisdom*
Ellsworth Jaeger

*Tiny House Designing, Building, & Living (Idiot's Guides)*
Gabriella and Andrew Morrison

*Stalking the Wild Asparagus*
Euell Gibbons

*The Forager's Guide to Wild Foods*
Nicole Apelian (PhD)

*Forager's Garden*
Samuel Thayer

## Acknowledgments

My Wife, Veronica
My Dad, Ray
Mr. Skamser (A+ English Teacher)
Dick Proeneke
Aldo Leopold
Larry Meiller (WPR Radio Host)

All the unsung good people around the world, working selflessly and tirelessly to keep us safe and healthy.

## My A-Team

Veronica Glidden, Editor-in-Chief
Anniken Fuller, Graphic Designer
   (annikencreative.com)
Maxwell Martinson, Editor, Journalist
Bruce Christianson, Photographer
Amy St. Mikael, Research Assistant

## My Mighty Proofers

Margaret Kelaart
Vicki Dischler
Chris Gamer
Wendy Nemitz
Darryl & Kathy Westlund
   (My Awesome Cuz's)

# APPENDIX

## A. Forth-To-Basics Plan - for going off-grid

- ○ Take stock of resources (money, materials, skills, tools, time)
- ○ Research everything, especially regulations. Ask questions of local authorities.
- ○ Find **land.**
- ○ Obtain a **rural address fire number** and **post office box** in town.
- ○ Establish a clearing and set up **campsite** with tent(s).
- ○ Purchase or borrow 4,000-watt gas-powered **generator.**
- ○ Set up 100-watt *Solar Roller* for charging batteries and phones.
- ○ Establish **driveway** from clearing to main road.
- ○ Scrounge and stockpile free or cheap **building materials.**
- ○ Install **sand-point well** (may require permit) and/or buy **water.**
- ○ Obtain a private sewer system permit (even for an outhouse).
- ○ Build **outhouse** (aka biff, privy or loo).
- ○ Obtain building permit for shelter (if necessary).
- ○ Build **shelter** (solid, sealed and rain-proof).
- ○ Install **wood stove** with rain-capped stack.
- ○ Install **CO/smoke detectors** and mount **fire extinguishers.**
- ○ Cut-n-split (or purchase) 3 cords **firewood** for first winter.
- ○ Persevere through first winter, gathering more firewood if needed.
- ○ Plant victory **garden.**
- ○ Install **rainwater** collection system for washing and watering.
- ○ Install modest **solar** system.
- ○ Rest.

## B. Looking for Land In Wisconsin

https://dnr.wisconsin.gov/topic/SmallBusiness/PurchaseLand.html

Below is a list of helpful information for those interested in buying land in Wisconsin. Other States may have similar programs and restrictions. Local zoning regulations at the county or township level may contain additional restrictions. Be sure to check the county's website and talk to local officials.

There may be issues related to water, soil, plants and animals on the property. Current or previous uses of the land, or any materials left behind may impact future use and should be considered before making a purchase.

**Country Acres:** A Guide to Buying and Managing Rural Property is available from the University of Wisconsin-Extension.

**The American Bankers Association** has developed 15 questions to ask before purchasing farmland.

**The University of Wisconsin-Extension** provides help to the agricultural community. Their Agriculture and Natural Resources page has a variety of resources including information on current agricultural issues and useful links to many other agricultural topics.

**Fast Tools - from the University of Illinois Center for Farm Finance Management** includes tools for land purchase analysis.

**The Chicago Federal Reserve** provides a lot of land data. You may want to compare the land you are considering with the information on their website.

**County land conservation departments** are the primary contacts for assisting landowners with these standards and prohibitions and can provide technical assistance and information regarding available funding. A list of county contacts is available in the Land & Water Conservation Directory.

**Financial Assistance**

**Wisconsin's Managed Forest Law** (MFL)

**A Program Summary**

**Forestry Assistance Locator**

**Forest Crop Law** (FCL) is another property tax incentive program for owners of forested land.

**Wisconsin Forest Landowner Grant Program.** This cost sharing program allows for reimbursing a landowner up to 50% of eligible costs incurred for non-commercial activities to protect and enhance forested land, prairies and water. A DNR forester can help develop a plan. Wisconsin Forest Landowner Grant Program.

# NOTES

"

*Now that I've shared the basics of our off-grid lifestyle, let's zoom out once more to the big picture of our little blue Earthship. Folks are concerned about the future of the planet and many are doing something about it by taking action. I predict that many more will join.*

*Keep in mind, we have the power as a species to make great progress as long as we learn from our collective mistakes as well as from our successes. A new world awaits, but what kind of world has yet to be determined. Will cooler heads prevail? We'll see.*

*Earth Riders of today and tomorrow should continue to seek and strive for balance with nature, especially while seeking our dreams. Let's determinedly go forth to basics while keeping our balance. I wish you the best of luck on your exciting journey!*

***Inspiration. Pass it on!*** — David R. Welder

*Love Your Earth*
© 2005 David R. Welder
Model: Wani Parks

# AUTHOR

David R. Welder is a multi-talented author with experience in the fields of environmental protection, energy conservation, photography, woodworking and off-grid living. After pursuing careers in the big city, he set off with his wife Veronica to live off-grid in rural Wisconsin. Now, he's laying down his unique perspectives, giving readers a straight, clear path to living off-grid. This book serves as a guide, posing questions, offering insights, and providing solutions to common challenges that come when you set forth and get back to basics.

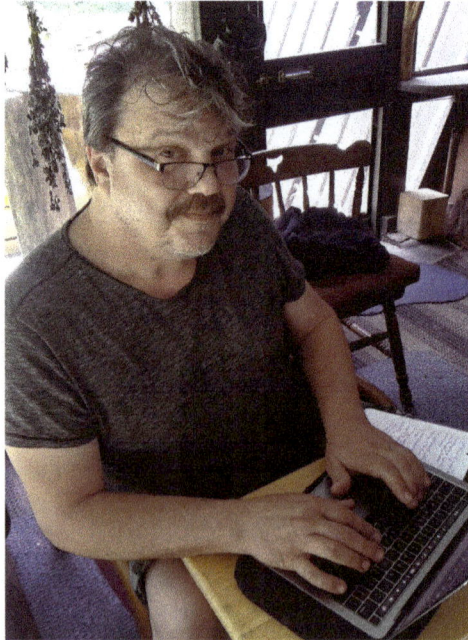

www.ingramcontent.com/pod-product-compliance
Lightning Source LLC
Chambersburg PA
CBHW052117030426
42335CB00025B/3021